CW00541978

♏

SCORPIO

SCORPIO

Let your Sun sign show you the way to a happy and fulfilling life

Marion Williamson & Pam Carruthers

This edition published in 2021 by Arcturus Publishing Limited
26/27 Bickels Yard, 151–153 Bermondsey Street, London SE1 3HA

ISBN: 978-1-83940-146-6
AD008766UK

Printed in China

CONTENTS

Introduction

Welcome, Scorpio! You have just taken a step toward what might become a lifelong passion. When astrology gets under your skin, there's no going back. Astrology helps you understand yourself and the people around you, and its dazzling insights become more fascinating the deeper you go.

Just as the first humans turned to the life-giving Sun for sustenance and guidance, your astrological journey begins with your Sun sign of Scorpio. First, we delve deeply into the heart of what makes you tick, then we'll continue to unlock your cosmic potential by exploring love, your career and health, the places you have an affinity with, and how you get along with family and friends.

Then it's over to gifted astrologer, Pam Carruthers, for her phenomenal birthdate analysis, where she gives detailed personality insights for every single specific Scorpio birthday.

In the last part of the book we get right inside how astrology works by revealing the different layers that will help you understand your own birth chart and offer the planetary tools to get you started.

Are you ready, Scorpio? Let's see if there's any truth to your ruthless, sexy reputation ...

CUSP DATES FOR SCORPIO

24 October – 22 November

The exact time of the Sun's entry into each zodiac sign varies every year, so it's impossible to list them all. If you were born a day either side of the dates above, you're a 'cusp' baby. This means you may feel like you're a blend of Scorpio/Libra or Scorpio/Sagittarius, or you may instinctively just know that you're one sign right to your core.

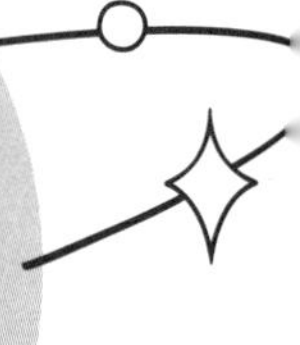

Going deeper

If you want to know once and for all whether you're a Libra, Scorpio or Sagittarius, you can look up your birthdate in a planetary ephemeris, of which there are plenty online. (See page 102 for more information.) This shows the exact moment the Sun moved into a new zodiac sign for the month you were born.

The Scorpio personality

Your reputation precedes you, Scorpio. Hypnotic, sexy and mysterious with that violent sting in your tail – you appear to have all of the zodiac's most extreme and exciting personality traits. But where do these dark and dubious characteristics come from, and do you actually deserve that reputation?

Scorpio is a Water sign, which is associated with strong emotions. Your planetary ruler is deep, dark, powerful Pluto, the lord of the underworld, controlling all that lies below the surface. The positive side of Pluto is that he pulls things from the dark into the light, so they can be transformed and healed. The darker side of Pluto reveals an obsession with power and control, which brings up deep passions: possessiveness, jealousy and revenge. Like your zodiac symbol, the Scorpion, you prefer to hide yourself and keep your motives secret, but you will strike if you are threatened.

WHAT LIES BENEATH

Enmeshed in dark myths and dramatic life-or-death symbolism, it's forgivable to imagine Scorpio to be heartless and cruel. But your tough exterior is just armour that protects your deeply sensitive Water sign heart. You feel your emotions very deeply, but you won't let just anyone see you vulnerable. You have a knack for unearthing other people's emotional weak spots and remembering just where to hurt them if they betray you in future. So, no, you won't display your softer side, at least not without a reciprocal exchange of vulnerabilities. It's a little like owning a nuclear deterrent. When you really trust someone, they'll know where you hurt, and you'll know where they hurt. If one of you pushes the other's button, you'll destroy each other. But it takes you a long time to get to that stage of trust.

SECRETS AND TRUST

You project an almost deadpan expression, appearing extremely well-controlled, intelligent and cool as a cucumber. But a particularly observant person will notice little signs that you're covering something up. White knuckles perhaps, tension in the jaw, perhaps a slight tremor in the voice if you're really upset. But there won't usually be much to allude to the boiling mass of lava-hot feelings you're just about managing to control.

You're a secretive person and it serves you well. When you gain someone's trust you take it as an honour. If a friend wishes to share that they're actually a spy or enjoy dressing up as a chicken for kicks, you'll take this knowledge to the grave. You keep secrets because knowledge is power, and, who knows – you may need to use it against them one day. But much more likely, you keep schtum because trust is everything to you. That's why you rely on so few people yourself. You'll enjoy hearing salacious gossip as much as anyone, but you treat real secrets with the utmost respect … and you will have a few of your own.

THE POWER OF MONEY

Scorpio is one of the financial zodiac signs, the other being your opposite number, Taurus. As a Pluto person you respect the power of money and your relationship to it can be complicated. You're smart and shrewd, and you tend to make money easily, and Scorpio is also associated with inheritance, so you may benefit from a legacy of some sort. You're quite secretive about how much money you make and won't be the one in the office discussing your annual bonus or how much your salary went up or down. But you'll be very interested in what other people are earning.

You have refined tastes and have an eye for luxury goods – you'll know expensive artwork, cars or antiques when you see them, and may even splash out on some investment pieces yourself. You're not usually a careless spender, and you'll feel quite anxious if you're digging into a credit card. You understand exactly what money can buy and safety and financial security are two of your top priorities. You often have a certain amount in the bank that you don't allow yourself to fall below – and you're self-controlled enough to stick to your guns.

Where a Sagittarian may plead poverty on a night out, and will actually be down to their last penny, you may claim you're struggling too, but you won't really be in the same boat. You'll probably have paid for your home outright and have a cosy bank balance and an impressive pension. But that's your private business, nobody else's.

In a personal birth chart, the eighth house is ruled by Scorpio, and it's the area connected with 'death, sex and other people's money'... again – always with the drama! You are considered more likely than most to benefit from joint financial ventures, or you may excel in careers where you look after other people's resources, taxes or pensions.

LOVE, PAIN AND POWER

Although quietly composed on the surface, you have tremendous reserves of emotional energy that make you ambitious and unrelenting. When you commit to a person, an idea or a job, you give it all you have and expect to come out on top. You have strong desires and there's an intensity to your feelings that others rarely experience. Where a Leo may stew over a comment that bruised their ego, they'll forget it later the same day in the spirit of forgiveness and optimism. You, on the other hand, may feel like you've been personally attacked and can seethe for days.

Every feeling you have is enhanced by your Water-driven nature, and jealousy is a particularly difficult emotion for Scorpio. If your lover causes you emotional pain, you will feel betrayed in a way that's hard for you to accept. You let someone into your inner sanctum – and they betrayed you. The lack of control over what's happening to you will be quite intolerable, and revenge will only seem fair. You are quite capable of cleanly and completely cutting people from your life.

You're not frightened of your emotions, but because you feel them so keenly, you are often at their mercy. You're not an escapist, and you know for sure the only way to tackle uncomfortable emotions is to do the hardest thing of all, you must face the source of the pain, bring it to its knees, look in its eyes, and then ask it honestly what it needs. You don't sugar-coat anything, especially when it comes to your own feelings. To you, there's no point in lying because you're just hiding from yourself. You can take it, and many Scorpios find themselves in counselling, locating the source of their troubles, so they can master their pain and avoid similar situations in future. You hate that others can have so much control over you but eventually you transform whatever brought you pain into a source of power. And that's why you always win!

OBSESSIVE AND SEXY

When you get interested in a subject, idea or a person, you become quite obsessive. You're the person that binge watches episodes of a dark, gripping TV series, who stays up all night reading an absorbing detective story or the one who has a sudden fascination with hypnosis or mysticism. Unlike most, you don't seem to get bored – only more interested. This addictive quality can also seep into your love life, where you may become obsessed by someone you know or, occasionally, a complete stranger.

But your fascination with sex isn't purely physical. You long to merge with someone else, to be possessed and lose your sense of individuality in a uniting of souls, to be reborn again. You don't just want sex, you're on a quest to attain a higher level of consciousness. No pressure on your partner then!

TAURUS LESSON

We often share characteristics with our opposite sign of the zodiac. Yours is Taurus, who understands your need to feel safe and secure, plus neither of you need to say much to know how the other is feeling. There's a smouldering intensity between you, a languid, simmering burn. You're both deeply passionate creatures but, until a spark lands, you both prefer to quietly size each other up and watch. Taurus and Scorpio are also the two financial signs of the zodiac. Taurus values their own talents and ability to get money, but Scorpio teaches Taurus that merging resources with others can bring more power and stability. Taurus teaches you serenity, how to let go of intense emotional attachment, and just be at peace with simple pleasures – beauty, harmony and comfort. You want to plumb the depths to find meaning and value, while Taurus just knows and embodies it.

Scorpio **Motto**

SOME OF THE BEST MOMENTS OF YOUR LIFE ARE THE ONES YOU CAN'T TELL ANYONE ABOUT.

Scorpio in love

In love you're all or nothing. Pluto-ruled people aren't wishy-washy or coy, but you have undeniable sex appeal. You're sultry and moody and when you're attracted to someone new, you hint at the passionate depths you're usually so keen to conceal. Your clothes tend to be plain in darker colours, but you choose sensual fabrics with a touch of drama, a subtle shine, velvet trim or an upturned collar. But it's your alluring, magnetic eyes that really draw people in. Sometimes your intensity can make people feel a little uncomfortable, but it's not intentional. You look directly into people's eyes for a fraction too long, often quite unconsciously, because that's where you discover their most precious secrets. Some people feel exposed in your gaze, while others enjoy feeling seen.

STILL WATERS RUN DEEP

Seductive but subtle, when you're attracted to someone your feelings will be strong, but you probably won't want to show your hand for a while. You like to watch from afar, noticing all the intimate details of the person who has captured your attention. You take in the way they move, how they use their hands when they speak and the timbre of their voice. You may be having a conversation, but you've lost the thread because you've been staring at their knees, neck or lips and wondering what it would be like to kiss them. You may try to keep your feelings to yourself, but your eyes will give you away. You have a hypnotic intensity when you're looking at someone you want, and that longing stare may reveal your real feelings.

You'll be looking for signs of reciprocation, but because you're so subtle, the other person may have only picked up the hint of a vibe. Unless you have Fire sign planets in your birth chart, who declare their feelings honestly and boldly, or you have loquacious Air sign placements that help you find the words to get your message across, your love interest may not be entirely sure what is going on. A more pure Scorpio tactic is to wait and watch, and hope they feel it too.

SEX: TRUST OR BUST

You take love seriously and don't make it easy for others to get close to you. The trust and security must be real before you let down your defences. As the zodiac's most passionate sign, you give yourself to your partner completely. For you sex isn't purely physical, it's an all-consuming, profound spiritual union and a release of powerful reserves of emotional energy. This is not something you take lightly as your lover will see you at your most vulnerable, so you will need plenty of reassurance that this will last forever.

Contrary to your reputation as a philanderer, you have a deep need for security and permanence in your relationships. Sex *is* essential to you, but you're no flash in the pan. If the love is real, you commit every fibre of your being to your partner loyally and, at times, almost obsessively. You can become possessive of your partner if they give cause to make you feel insecure, and can become very jealous, if provoked. But emotionally, you give everything, so if your partner cheats, shames you or breaks your heart, you will want revenge. And the best revenge of all is to find a way not to care.

TRICKY EMOTIONS

You work harder than any other zodiac sign to repair yourself if you've been emotionally wounded. Because you are so brave and honest with yourself, you have the power to regenerate, heal and to put yourself back stronger than before. But, in order to be reborn, first you have to die. You do this by fully experiencing your pain, re-living it, feeling the emotions as fully as possible, giving yourself over to the truth of the loss, rejection, fear or anger. You go deep into the well of feeling, then you analyse yourself over and over for a way through. You don't always find easy answers, and sometimes there are none, but eventually, sometimes after many years, you come

Most compatible love signs

Cancer – sensitive, intuitive Cancer can provide you with the security and reassurance you seek and can read your changing moods.

Taurus – The Taurean languid, slow, sensuous approach to life masks inner passions that attract and intrigue you.

Capricorn – responsible, steady goat people won't spring any surprises on you emotionally, and they're usually quite sensible with money.

Least compatible love signs

Libra – you're too hot to handle for superficial Libra who likes things to be nice rather than terrifyingly passionate and sweaty.

Leo – the king of brash meets the king of subtle – you're made of different stuff and won't see eye to eye for long.

Aries – you like the self-belief and boldness of Aries, but they lack your emotional finesse, which you can find quite annoying.

Scorpio at work

Strong-willed and magnetic, you're a motivated self-starter with an aura of mystery. Perfectly self-controlled, you never give away what you're thinking and, if you can help it, you won't rely on anyone else to help you get your work done. You're a bit of a loner in your job, disliking being in the spotlight, and your co-workers may even be a little suspicious of you. But that's just because you give them so little to go on.

You keep your personal life tightly zipped and have something of a stiffly buttoned persona. However, your composure is deceptive, for you are a compassionate, kind and caring Water sign. Workmates who have taken time to get to know you better, sense your empathy and discretion, and may find themselves spilling their hearts to you. You love discovering what makes other people tick, and you're a wonderful listener. Trustworthy to your core, any gossip that finds its way to your desk will be kept strictly to yourself.

SCORPIO CAREERS

Discreet, professional and intuitive, any work where you have to research, analyse or dig deep to discover more information will suit your detective brain. You don't mess with trivialities – you get right down to business and are excellent at intuiting what's really going on with people and how they really feel under the surface. Employment that involves consumer psychology, counselling or any element of negotiation, suits your love of getting to the heart of what really motivates people. Scorpio, along with Taurus, is one of the zodiac's financial signs. Where Taurus understands how to make money and build on it, Scorpio has a talent for merging with others in money-making ventures. You would find banking, accounting, estate agency, or any position where you make a commission from other people's investments, very satisfying.

SCORPIO AT THE TOP

If you've made it to the top of your profession, and dynamic, ambitious Scorpios usually do, you'll probably have a bit of a reputation for being something of a ruthless negotiator. You never let on about what you really want until after you have it, so your business moves are often cloaked in secrecy.

There's no problem you can't solve, and your professional manner demands respect without ever asking for it. You rarely raise your voice to anyone in your charge, but there's an edge to you that suggests you might. You appear unemotional to the point of coldness but, very occasionally, and usually because of a breach of privacy or trust, you'll flip your lid.

The people around you won't quite believe you're the same person.

You give away little about your own life, yet you miss nothing about what your employees get up to. They'll have to be far more devious if they believe they can pull the wool over your eyes, and you'll spot when they're on social media or pretending to work when they're actually shopping.

You don't make a big deal of minor transgressions, but you'll create a mental note of them in case they come in useful at a later date. You don't want to rock the boat unless you have to, preferring to keep your energy – and everyone else's attention – on the job in hand. Your fabled Scorpio stinger is rarely seen in the workplace, though colleagues may gossip about that one legendary time when you allegedly punched the head of marketing, and you won't say anything to dispel the myth. But more likely, if you really take a dislike to someone, you'll just completely ignore them!

Most compatible colleagues

Sagittarius – unlike you, Sagittarius is open and honest, and you know exactly who you're dealing with – and how to manipulate them!

Aries – these guys can be childish and aggressive, but you definitely want them on your side in a fight or competition.

Virgo – you respect the modest, conscientious Virgo manner. You know if the pair of you work together that you're a quietly devastating team.

Least compatible colleagues

Scorpio – you tolerate each other if you're working toward the same goal, but if you're enemies, forget it; you'll both perish trying to outmanoeuvre each other.

Aquarius – great fun to be around and have genius ideas, but they're unlikely to respect your authority.

Leo – talk too much, need too much praise, and can't work unsupervised.

Perfect Scorpio Careers

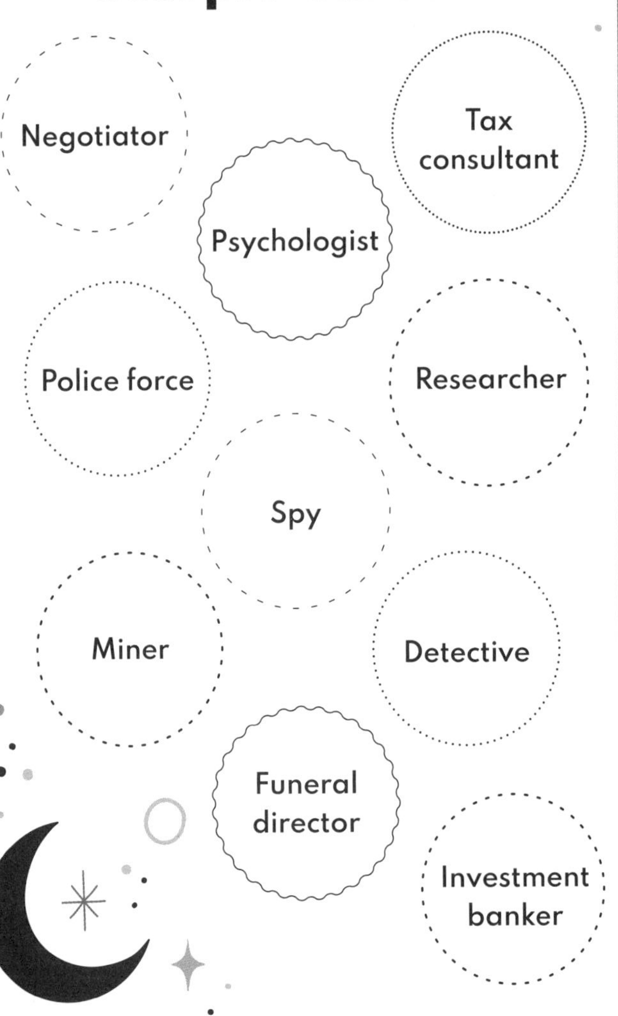

Scorpio

Work Ethic

THE ONLY PEOPLE I OWE MY LOYALTY TO ARE THOSE WHO NEVER MADE ME QUESTION THEIRS.

Scorpio friends and family

You're usually self-contained enough to feel quite happy in your own company and you don't see the point of maintaining acquaintances unless there's a compelling reason. You don't need a companion on shopping trips or to gossip with over coffee. So, when you do form a new friendship, that person will probably already have a shared interest or be especially interesting to you.

You can be terrifyingly honest with your pals: if they ask your opinion, they should be prepared to handle the answer. Some may be offended by your bluntness, but it's your authenticity that also makes your opinion so sought after. You find flattery quite suspicious, and will put your feelers out for ulterior motives, so you wouldn't dream of being the bearer of empty compliments.

Some mistake your seriousness and dislike of giving praise as unfriendly, but they'd be missing out on what having a true friend really means. When you are committed, that's it, they have your heart. You make friends for life and you will fiercely support and defend people you care about. You're just not into the conventional social niceties – things like baby showers, housewarming parties and coffee mornings. But when it really matters, you'll be there. You're a strong shoulder to cry on and you always offer the sincerest advice. And if your friend has royally messed up, you won't judge and you'll even stump up the metaphorical bail money.

You might be a little antisocial at times, and you can be weirdly secretive, but you do enjoy listening to your friends' woes and are spookily able to pinpoint exactly what they're going through. Your heart is soft under all that shiny, black, armour, but you let people see the real you through your uncanny empathy and kindness. There's no better friend to share painful truths with and feel understood on a soul-deep level.

SCORPIO AT HOME

Scorpio homes can be a little bare looking, decidedly flounce-free and stark. You don't quite sleep on a bed of nails, but you like a sleek, shiny, sexy style – something that's easy to keep clean while being dramatic and ordered. You're not a collector and neither are you sentimental, so you don't choose to display mementos or many photographs of fuzzy moments together. Your secret treasures – erotic letters, pictures of past loves and sexy messages – lie hidden in drawers, locked boxes, laptops and deep in the attic; they are for your eyes only.

SCORPIO PARENT

Passionate and sensitive to your child's needs, you have an almost telepathic bond with your progeny. You may be on the controlling side, suspicious of who your kid gets involved with, or – when they're older – where they're going, but it comes from a deeply protective instinct. Nobody messes with your kids ... nobody apart from you that is!

SCORPIO CHILD

Scorpio kids' intuition is uncanny. They're not frightened of your more intense emotions, in fact, they'll find them more comforting than if you try and fake being happy. Their own emotional reactions can be very dramatic as they're so sensitive to changing atmospheres. But they also respond to love and kindness with heartbreakingly touching honesty.

Healthy Scorpio

Ruled by Pluto, the powerhouse planet of extremes, your metabolism is usually high. Your calm exterior masks your intensely emotional nature, which must have a healthy outlet, otherwise you can get tense and lose your cool – and nobody's comfortable with an annoyed Scorpio around!

One of the most important things you can do for your health is to talk to someone about your feelings. You have such a rich and intense emotional life, but you keep things very much to yourself. If you don't feel you can express yourself to a friend or partner, going for counselling or psychotherapy will be a therapeutic experience where you can safely bare your soul.

You rarely do half measures and can be quite obsessive about your health – as in taking things to excessive lengths. As the most self-controlled sign of the zodiac, you want to master your thoughts, emotions and your physical well-being. You're driven, energetic and competitive but you usually prefer to work out on your own. Extreme sports and adrenaline boosters such as rock climbing, skiing, cave diving and kite surfing will help you channel repressed or challenging feelings and relieve stress and help move any blocked energy.

FOOD AND DRINK

Your take-it-or-leave-it attitude sees you swing from being obsessed with one type of food to being off your kibbles completely. You tend to enjoy foods that others turn their nose up at – intense dark chocolate, bitter cocktails, and pungent blue cheeses. Spicy, hot, energy-giving foods such as curries, chilli and hot pepper sauce give you a satisfying kick, and you'll experiment with anything exotic, pungent or dark and delightful.

Scorpio's dark, moody, dangerous energy makes you the zodiac's 'sex, drugs, and rock'n'roll' character. This isn't so much for the escapism – you're far too self-aware for that – it's more in the spirit of curiosity and experimentation. A character of extremes, you can push things a little too far. You want to know what life is like on the wild side and you may sometimes end up in some darker places than you originally intended. But then you counter this by living like a monk for weeks after any serious blow-outs.

You may be a little obsessive about your weight and have probably already learned from experience that extreme or yo-yo dieting doesn't do you any good. You get 100% involved with what you're doing, so you have less trouble sticking to cabbage soup diets, ridiculously low-calorie plans or pineapple-only type fads. You can be too disciplined for a while, then ping the other way and live like King Henry VIII for a few weeks to make up for it. Finding a balance with food, drink and medicine may be a battle at times but you will master it eventually – as you do with everything! It is just a matter of time before you find your focus.

BODY AREA: SEXUAL ORGANS

You didn't get your hot-blooded notoriety from nowhere, Scorpio! Unsurprisingly, the part of the body you're associated with is the reproductive organs. A healthy sex life is a natural part of any Scorpio's well-being, offering emotional connection as well as a physical release.

Scorpio on the move

A creature of Plutonian extremes you're never really going to enjoy a wishy-washy vacation. You crave real experiences in challenging environments. You want to feel transformed and challenged, spiritually and physically, and to come home enriched. Trips that might scare the life out of your friends or family will be right up your street!

TRAVEL LIGHT

Disliking carrying baggage generally, you'd rather pack the bare essentials. If you could leave for the airport in the clothes you're wearing right now, with a penknife, passport and bottle opener, that would be perfect. You can wash your pants in the sink, steal other people's toiletries and brush your teeth with sandpaper if you have to – you will get by.

You're happy travelling alone, but a companion would give you someone to compare your experience with and could also help sorting out the more prosaic aspects of your trip. You haven't got much patience for looking for good deals on flight and comparing accommodation prices. You're clever with money but you're rather someone else takes care of the details and you'll happily pay a bit extra to avoid doing that yourself!

Even if you're off on a beach holiday with a few friends, you'll secretly have a goal to come back home in better shape physically, mentally or spiritually. A yoga mat, skipping rope or self-help book will find its way into your suitcase long before essentials like passports, mosquito repellent or glamorous outfits.

SCORPIO HEAVEN

You want your time away to really mean something. Lying on the beach every day might be relaxing but it doesn't really touch you on an emotional level. For that you'll need to test yourself in some way. You rival Virgo for the zodiac sign that's hardest on themselves and most likely to enjoy a steep learning curve when you take a break from everyday life. Adventures where you discover something new about yourself will be high on your list.

Silent retreats, the more spartan the better, help you tune into what's really going on with you deep inside – even better if these are held in remote or dramatic locations. Fasting detox breaks appeal as you'll get a kick out of testing your self-control and if there's a coffee enema included, all the better! But the most Scorpio thing you could do is to embark upon a shamanic journeying quest or to undertake a week-long course in deep psychotherapy – both will likely change you on a fundamental level and fulfil your desire to attain another level of consciousness altogether.

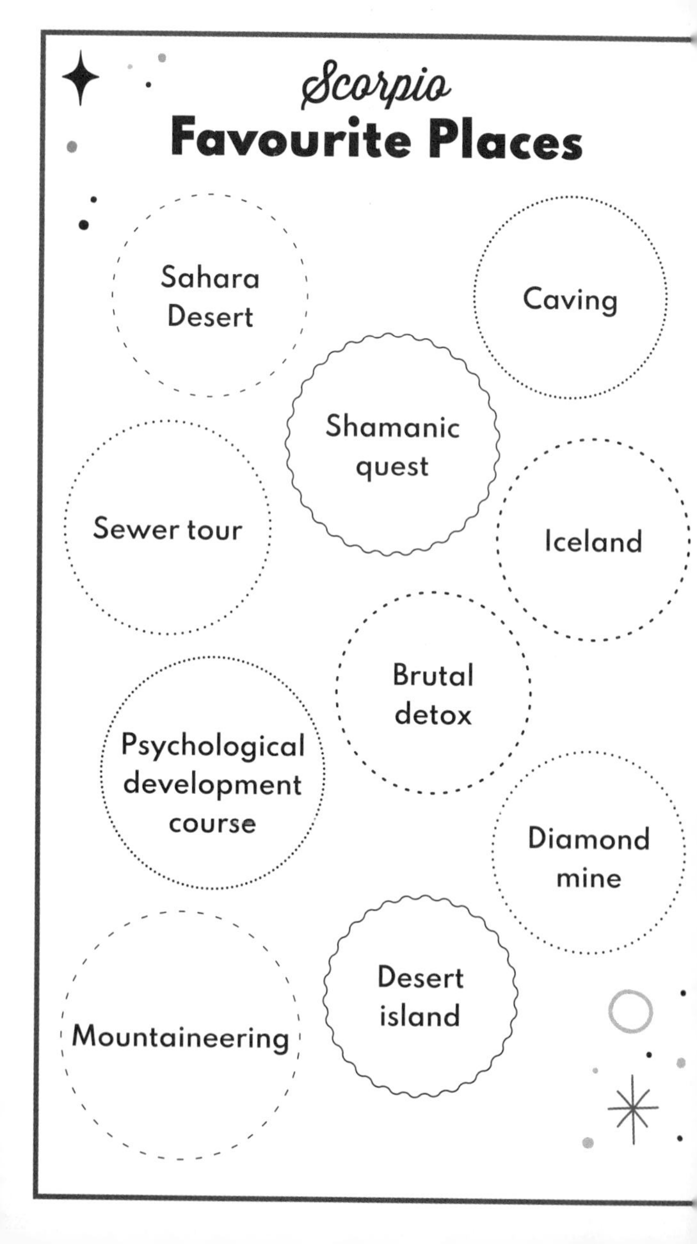
Scorpio
Favourite Places
Sahara Desert
Caving
Shamanic quest
Sewer tour
Iceland
Brutal detox
Psychological development course
Diamond mine
Desert island
Mountaineering

Scorpio

Travel Ethic

A SMALL BAG AND A BIG TRIP MAKE FOR A LIFE-CHANGING ADVENTURE!

Scorpio
BIRTHDATE
PERSONALITIES

Discover your
personal forecast
for the day of
your birth.

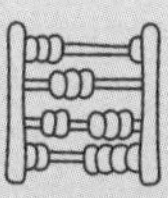

24 October

You are a practical and passionate person with a strong sense of duty. You can cheerfully do the most routine and repetitive tasks – if you are in love with what you do, and if you feel it offers value to others. There is an aura of quiet dedication about you and you are more than happy to work alone. You are the archetypal planner; you love systems and calculate everything down to the last detail. This creates a lack of spontaneity and really annoys your impatient friends! You can be stubborn and certainly won't be pushed around. The first impression you give potential lovers is of a self-controlled and modest person, but in private you are a very romantic and tactile lover. Fitness is a priority and running while listening to a self-improvement audio book combines your two loves.

STRENGTHS
Grounded, amorous
WEAKNESSES
Obstinate and, at times, inhibited
MEDITATION
It's okay to let yourself go, as long as you can get yourself back.

25 October

You are a charismatic person with immense panache and passion. You have a vivid imagination and an artistic fervour that you need to express through a creative medium. This could be through drama or another intense art form which becomes your career. People and relationships govern your entire life and you have a huge need to be liked. This can hinder you, since pleasing people is not possible all of the time. You sometimes say yes when you mean no, and then don't deliver on a promise, so you end up – inadvertently – upsetting people. Romance and love take priority, and you are happiest being with just one person. With your innate sense of style and grace, ballroom dancing with your partner is the ideal exercise and a great way to spend quality time with them.

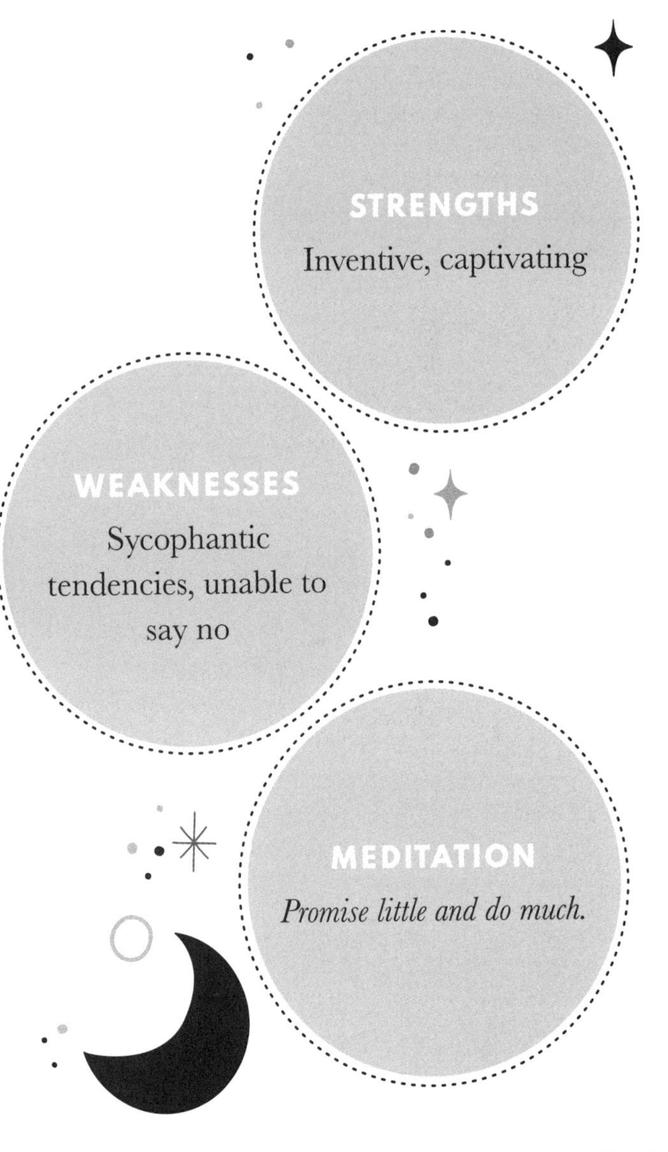

STRENGTHS

Inventive, captivating

WEAKNESSES

Sycophantic tendencies, unable to say no

MEDITATION

Promise little and do much.

26 October

You are a dynamic and powerful person with strong convictions. You are self-possessed and confident, with a formidable determination to succeed. In your life you have been tested and can face situations that others shrink from. You will gladly fight on behalf of the underdog and make a resolute campaigner on social issues. You have entrenched opinions on most subjects and can be incredibly stubborn. Committed to your purpose from a young age, your focus is on analysing and investigating any subject in depth. Superficiality annoys you immensely and you cannot tolerate fools. Your relationships are intense and you are fiercely loyal. Once committed, you are unshakeable and rarely give up on your partner. Shiatsu, deep tissue massage or acupressure would be highly beneficial as you hold a lot of tension in your body.

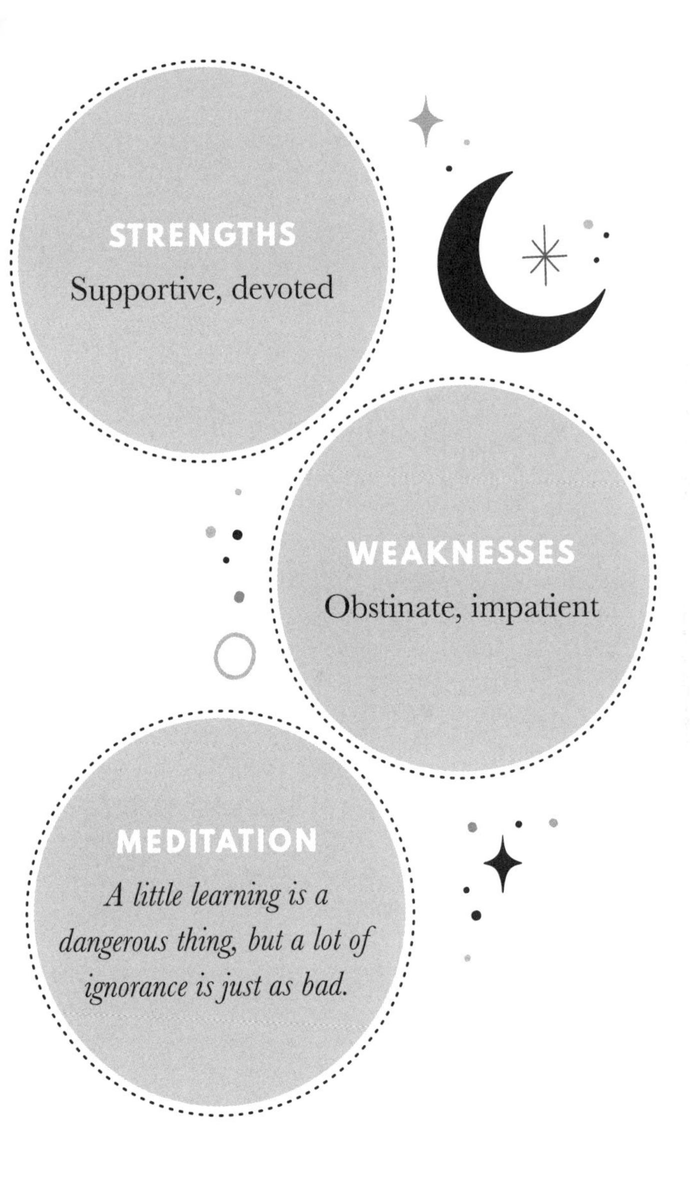

STRENGTHS

Supportive, devoted

WEAKNESSES

Obstinate, impatient

MEDITATION

A little learning is a dangerous thing, but a lot of ignorance is just as bad.

27 October

You are a passionate and outspoken person who needs a mission in life. Once found, your vision propels you forward and your commitment is strong. You are a philosopher, someone who adores discussing the meaning of life. Nothing shocks you and your natural optimism and good humour buoys others up in the face of trouble. You are a born psychologist and can develop into being an excellent teacher of your peers. You love travel and absorbing different cultures and could easily live abroad. You can be fanatical about your beliefs and tend to get on your soap box and alienate others – even without meaning to. That said, you are also very persuasive! Emotionally intense, your relationship is your bedrock, but you also need a lot of freedom. A night out at the theatre transports you into the fantasy world you yearn for.

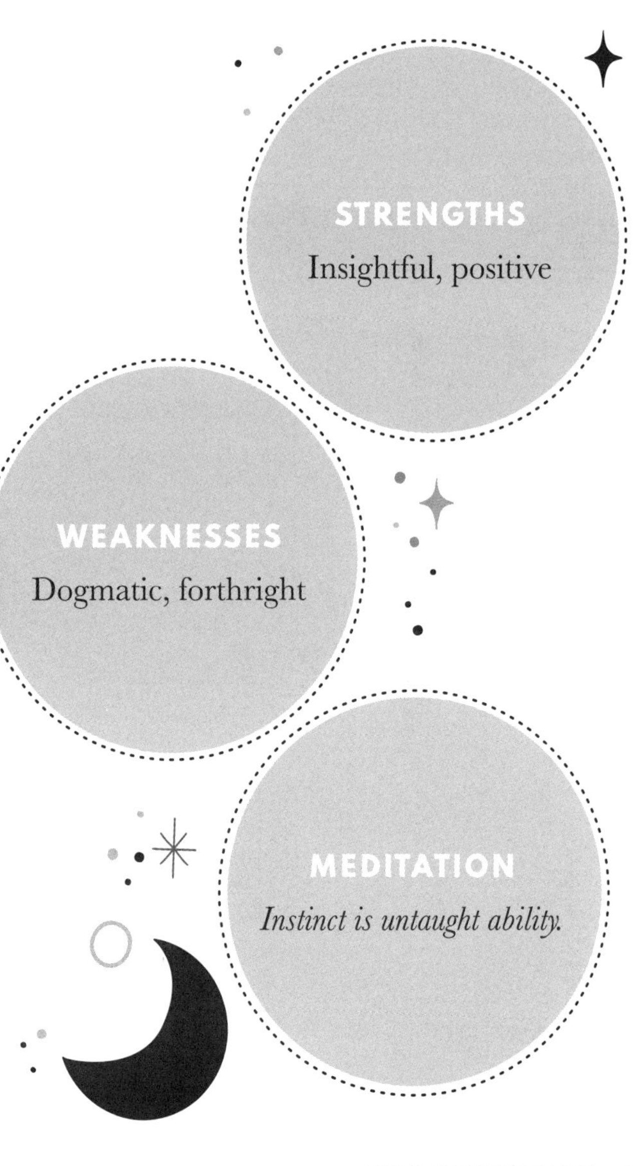
STRENGTHS
Insightful, positive
WEAKNESSES
Dogmatic, forthright
MEDITATION
Instinct is untaught ability.

28 October

You are a focused and determined person who believes work is of utmost importance. You know about the importance of goals and are willing to undergo lengthy training to improve your skills. You are tough and have true grit – nothing fazes you. You have extraordinary self-discipline and understand and obey the rules of society. You can expect too much from others and judge them if they don't come up to your high standards. With your strong convictions, the realm of politics is well suited to you, as is the law. You have an earnest and sombre outlook yet have a gift for satire and a dry wit. In love you tend to play hard-to-get, which is very alluring to the opposite sex. You tend to overwork so being frivolous, singing and playing music brings the balance you require for contentment.

STRENGTHS

Attentive, enticing

WEAKNESSES

Critical, tough

MEDITATION

If music be the food of love, play on.

29 October

You are an innovator, a distinctive person with unusual tastes and a strong desire for experimentation. In your life you are always pushing boundaries and are attracted to explore metaphysics and occult sciences. You love to analyse and dissect information and are able to grasp deep abstract concepts. Your ability to observe from a detached viewpoint makes you an excellent trouble shooter or arbitrator. In your personal life you value truth and honesty in all your relationships. With your lover you demand a lot of personal space yet also desire passion and closeness. You tend to withdraw and remove yourself emotionally when things get too intense, but you still want to remain friends. Exploring your deeper emotions with a therapist would be beneficial. Shiatsu is a good treatment to help shift your energy.

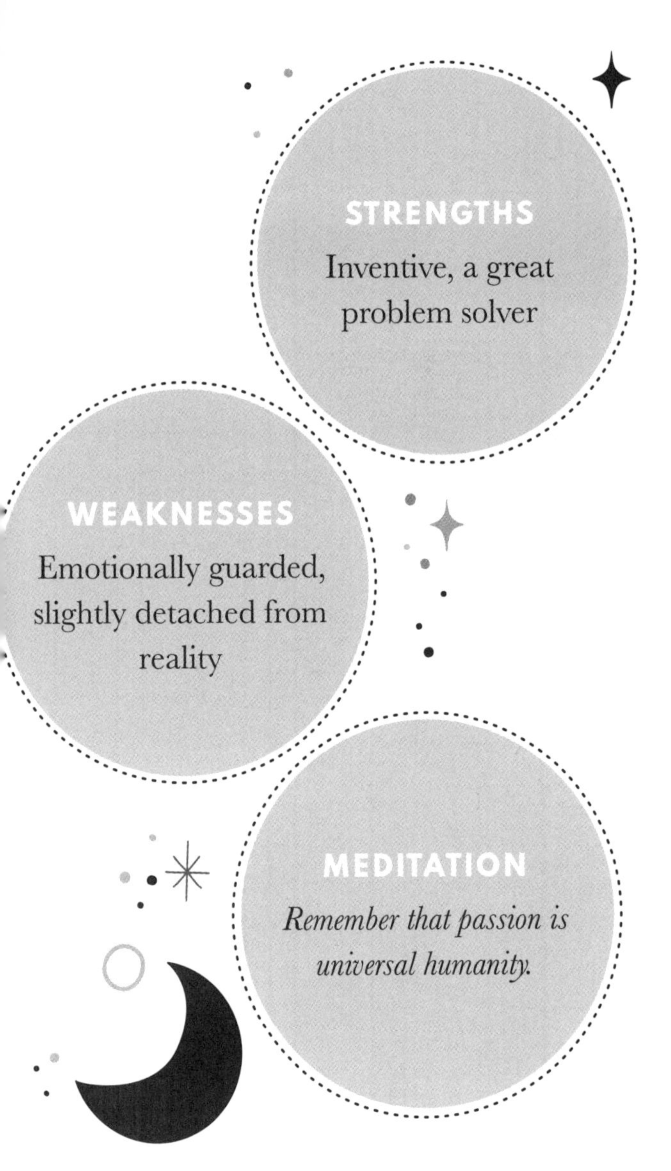

STRENGTHS

Inventive, a great problem solver

WEAKNESSES

Emotionally guarded, slightly detached from reality

MEDITATION

Remember that passion is universal humanity.

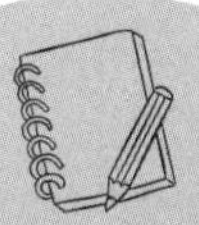

30 October

You are a playful and yet serious person who is bright and good-humoured one minute, then can be grave and sombre the next. Eternally youthful, you tend to look younger than you actually are. Your mind is intensely curious and you can dart from one topic to another. You are a gifted writer as you can articulate the deep emotions people feel, and you have the added ability to laugh at the darker side of life. In relationships you love variety, but this leads you to flit from one person to another. It takes a long time for you to settle down and yet you yearn for emotional security. As you mature you appreciate that having lots of friends with varied interests will keep you stimulated and entertain you. In this way you can synthesize these two aspects of your personality.

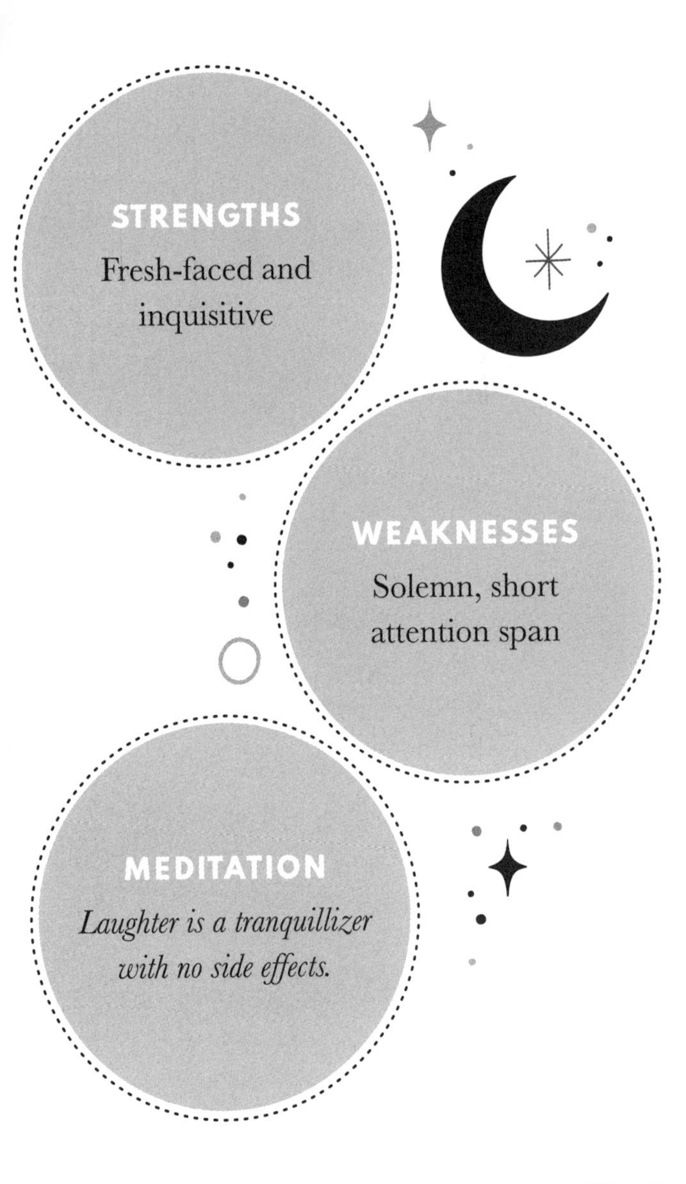
STRENGTHS
Fresh-faced and inquisitive
WEAKNESSES
Solemn, short attention span
MEDITATION
Laughter is a tranquillizer with no side effects.

31 October

You are a sensitive and impressionable person with a deep nostalgia for the past. Home and family are a central part of your life and you tend to be patriotic regarding your chosen country of residence. You seek success in life – you need to have a purpose and your choice of career is vitally important. Your concern for others propels you to help create change in people's lives, often through politics or working for a charity. In your personal life, once committed you give yourself totally. You are sensual and affectionate so your relationship needs to be deeply fulfilling. Your greatest desire is to be with someone who offers you the emotional security you crave and understands the depth of your feelings. You are an introspective person and can easily sink into a dark mood, but watching a romantic comedy will lighten you up.

STRENGTHS

Thoughtful and a born protector

WEAKNESSES

Prone to pessimism, too self-analysing

MEDITATION

It doesn't hurt to be optimistic. You can always cry later.

1 November

You are a champion and a passionate crusader with a strong will to succeed in life. You are a fighter and have enormous amounts of courage and emotional strength. You work with determination but can overdo it and exhaust yourself. You need a mission, a worthy cause to which you can dedicate yourself, heart and soul. You would do well in science or medicine as well as commerce, but whatever your work, you need to be constantly challenged and physically moving as you are impatient and restless if desk-bound. In relationships you love the thrill of the chase and, once you commit, you are a fiercely loyal partner. You need to release your pent-up emotions and a combative game such as ice hockey or squash is well suited to your temperament.

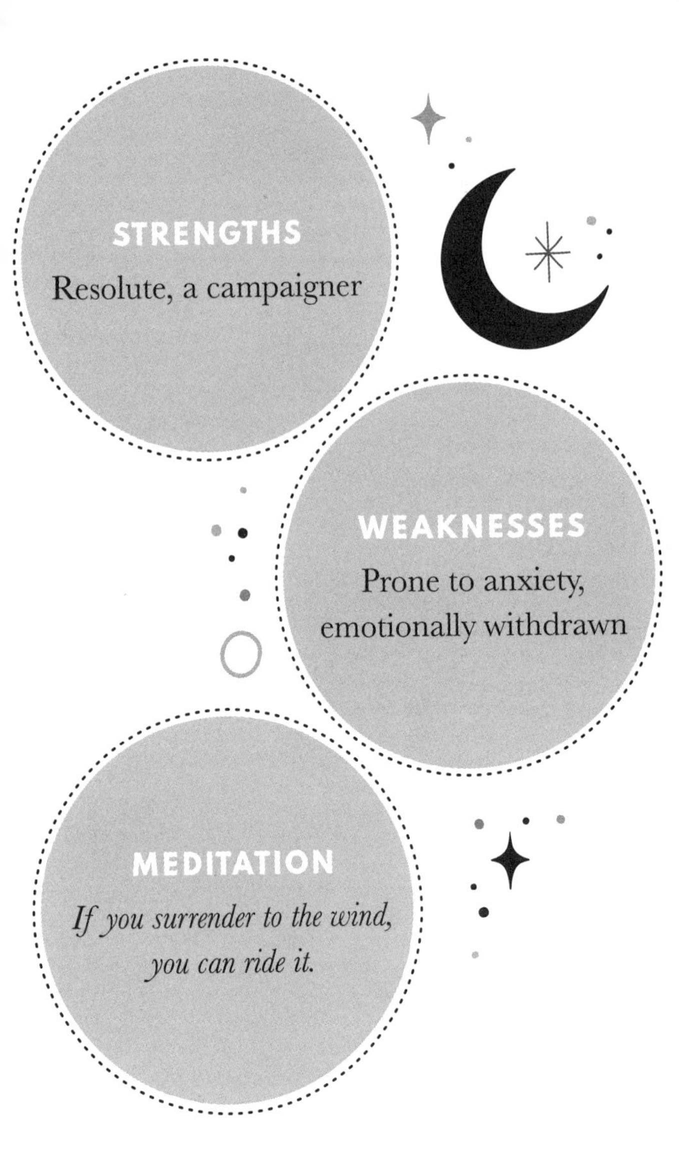
STRENGTHS
Resolute, a campaigner
WEAKNESSES
Prone to anxiety, emotionally withdrawn
MEDITATION
If you surrender to the wind, you can ride it.

2 November

You are a sensual but self-controlled person with shrewd business acumen and the ability to handle large amounts of money. You are essentially quiet and gentle and prefer to live in the countryside and commune with nature. There is also another side to you which thrives in the powerful world of politics or exploring the mysteries of archaeology. You work hard and play hard and love good food and wine. When stressed you can easily over-indulge, then put yourself on a strict regime of self-denial. In relationships you are strongly emotional or else so self-contained that your partner spends a lot of time trying to fathom what you are feeling. This tendency to withdraw is an old pattern, and it is a good idea to make an effort and communicate your inner world with your beloved.

STRENGTHS

Astute in business, good-natured

WEAKNESSES

Prone to excess, at times emotionally inhibited

MEDITATION

Self-confidence is the result of a successfully survived risk.

3 November

You are a quick-witted and cheerful person who is a social butterfly. You can be devastatingly witty and your humour verges on the absurd. This ability is brilliant for a career as a stand-up comic or a comedy scriptwriter. You are always ready with a joke, but this can be your way of avoiding deeper emotions, batting questions away with a witty response rather than letting people see your weaknesses. At times you are overly flippant and the odd comment can catch people off guard. You are passionate with an urge to explore the secrets of how the universe works, and studying astronomy and astrology would fulfil you. In love you can blow hot or cold and you like to keep your options open. Fancy dress is a wonderful way for you to unwind and to explore your own varied personality.

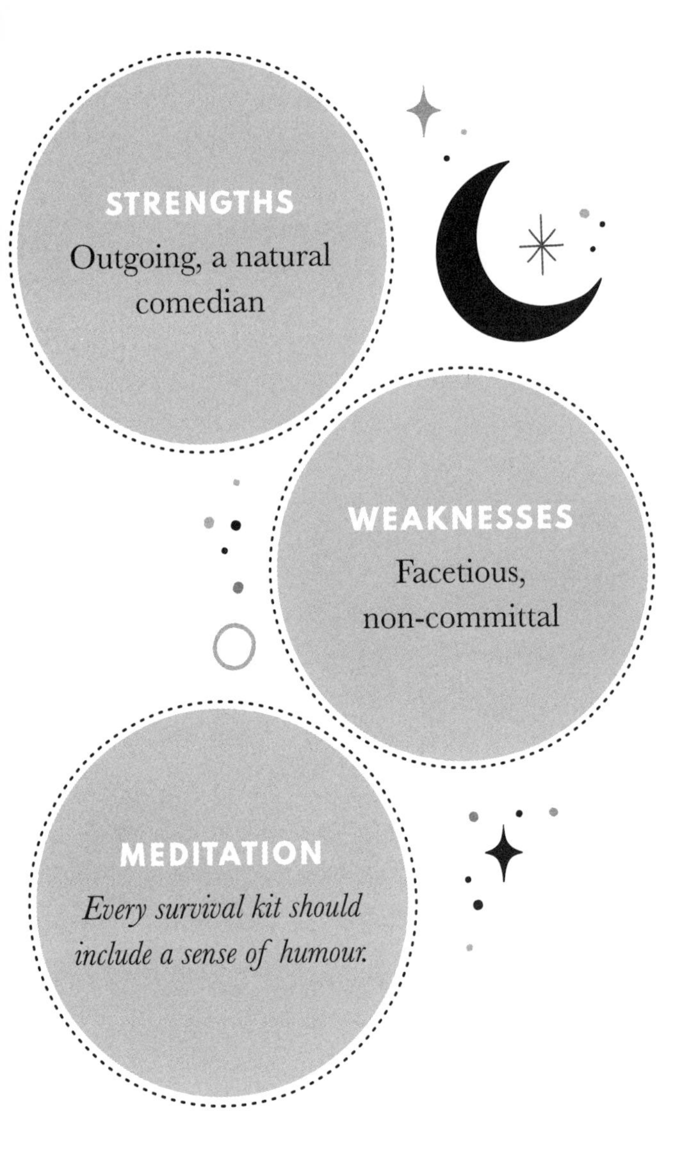
STRENGTHS
Outgoing, a natural comedian
WEAKNESSES
Facetious, non-committal
MEDITATION
Every survival kit should include a sense of humour.

4 November

You are a powerhouse of emotion, a person driven to explore the depths of the human condition and experience. You can swing from highs to extreme lows and sulk for weeks. You have an instinct for survival and can endure great emotional and physical pain. Your deep perceptiveness concerning other people, allied with your great intellect, would make you a superb psychologist or doctor. However, if stressed your strong feelings can take over and compel you to make irrational and overly subjective decisions. Early in life you learn to be self-sufficient and keep many emotions hidden from public view. If extremely provoked, you can explode into volcanic rage. Passion is your middle name so a relationship is essential. Choose wisely, as they need to receive, and give you, strong emotional support.

STRENGTHS

Intuitive, determined

WEAKNESSES

Unreasonable, short-tempered

MEDITATION

People who fly into a rage always make a bad landing.

5 November

You are an outrageous person with an enormous amount of magnetism. You succeed where others may fail as you have a determination that never gives up. Your need is for recognition, to be someone, and you will do anything to achieve that. However, once you are well known you can complain about the lack of privacy. You can end up wearing dark glasses in the depths of winter in order to hide and your car could end up having tinted windows! You are a superb business person who is attracted to working in the glamorous world of the media. A born romantic, you are an ardent lover and need a secure relationship to express your deepest emotions. As long as you are in charge all is well. You love to dress up for an occasion so a going to the theatre or opera – especially if you sit in a box – is perfect.

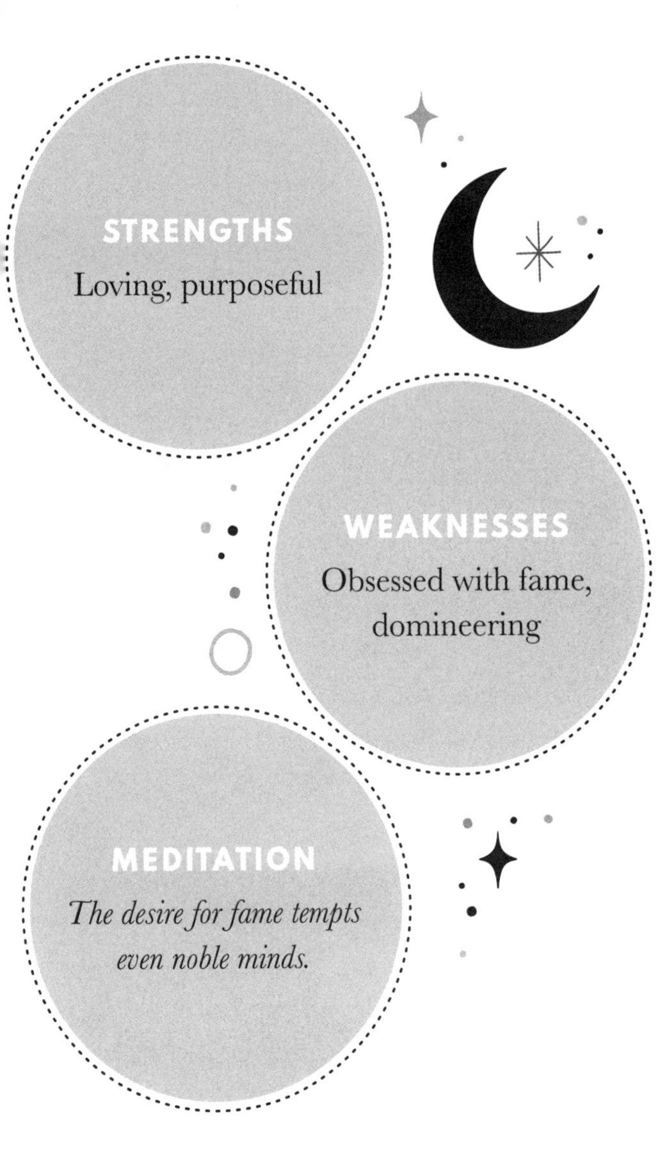
STRENGTHS
Loving, purposeful
WEAKNESSES
Obsessed with fame, domineering
MEDITATION
The desire for fame tempts even noble minds.

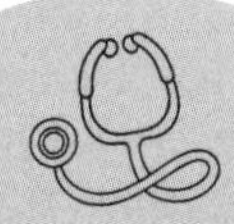

6 November

You are a conscientious and passionate person with a real need to be of service to others. Truly sympathetic to the human condition, you are naturally drawn to the healing professions. You have clear insight and a gift for analysing people and situations. Highly critical, at times your scathing honesty is just too much for others to handle, but as you age, you learn to soften your approach. You have a tendency to support the underdog and a charitable nature. Health and your diet are of constant concern and you often experiment with the latest health-food trends. You are a very physical person so your partner needs to give you lots of affection and hugs for you to feel loved. Walking in nature restores your inner balance as your mental processes can get overactive.

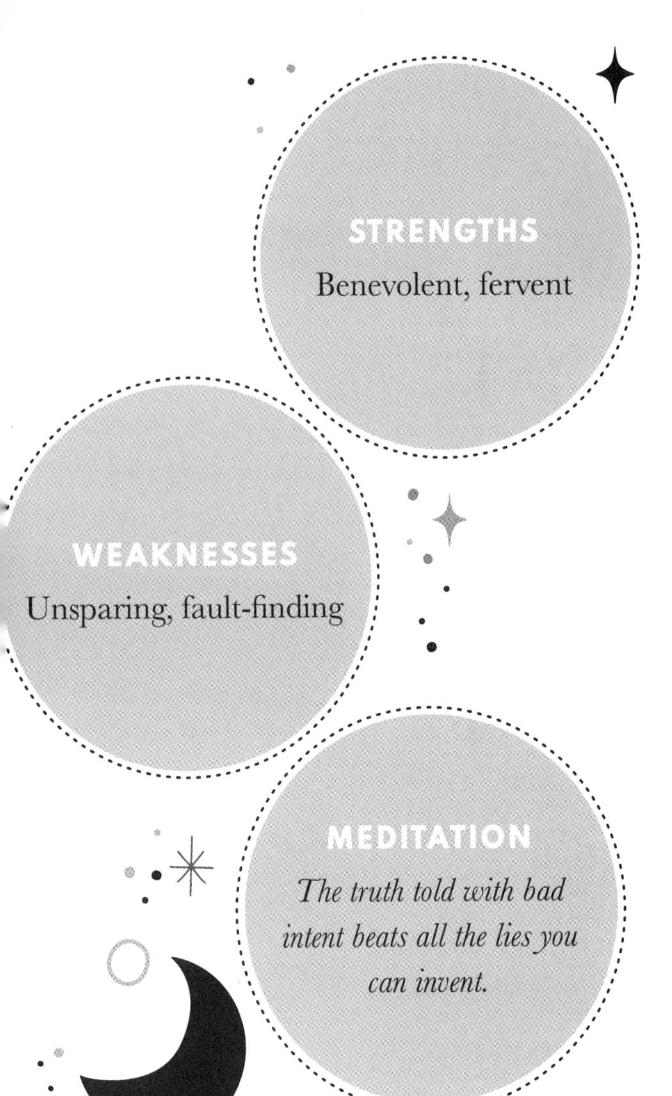
STRENGTHS
Benevolent, fervent
WEAKNESSES
Unsparing, fault-finding
MEDITATION
The truth told with bad intent beats all the lies you can invent.

7 November

You are an idealist, a graceful and intelligent person with both eloquence and charm. Well suited to the world of commerce, you have excellent negotiation skills and love creating peace and harmony. With an innate sense of fair play, injustice stirs you up to protest. You can be tough, and people can underestimate just how forceful you can be. You would do well in politics and management. If you feel insecure, you can be manipulative to get your own way. You need a close relationship to feel fulfilled and you are a passionate and romantic partner. You talk for hours on end with your beloved. However, if you compromise too much, you will end up fighting. Practising some form of martial arts or taking up fencing will benefit you immensely in releasing the aggression that you keep hidden.

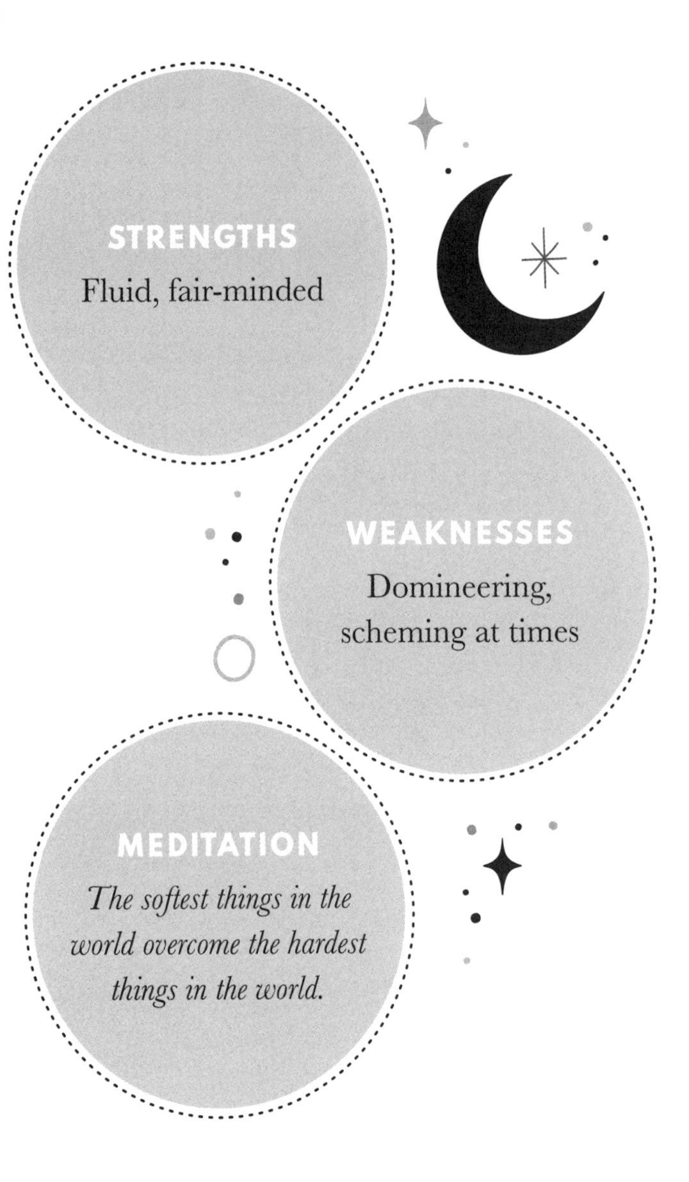

STRENGTHS

Fluid, fair-minded

WEAKNESSES

Domineering, scheming at times

MEDITATION

The softest things in the world overcome the hardest things in the world.

8 November

You are a quiet rebel, a person with strong desires and hidden depths. People find you mysterious and fascinating but they can feel that they never really know you completely. The mask you wear comes as a result of needing protection as you are very sensitive. You have a phenomenal memory and nothing is ever forgotten. This can be a real bonus if you are a writer, but it also means that you find it hard to let go of bad memories and heal old wounds. You can also be very controlling which makes for difficult business partnerships. In personal relationships you are devoted and steadfast, and expect your partner to be the same. Singing your heart out in private, or if your voice is good, at a karaoke night, is a wonderful way to release your pent-up energy.

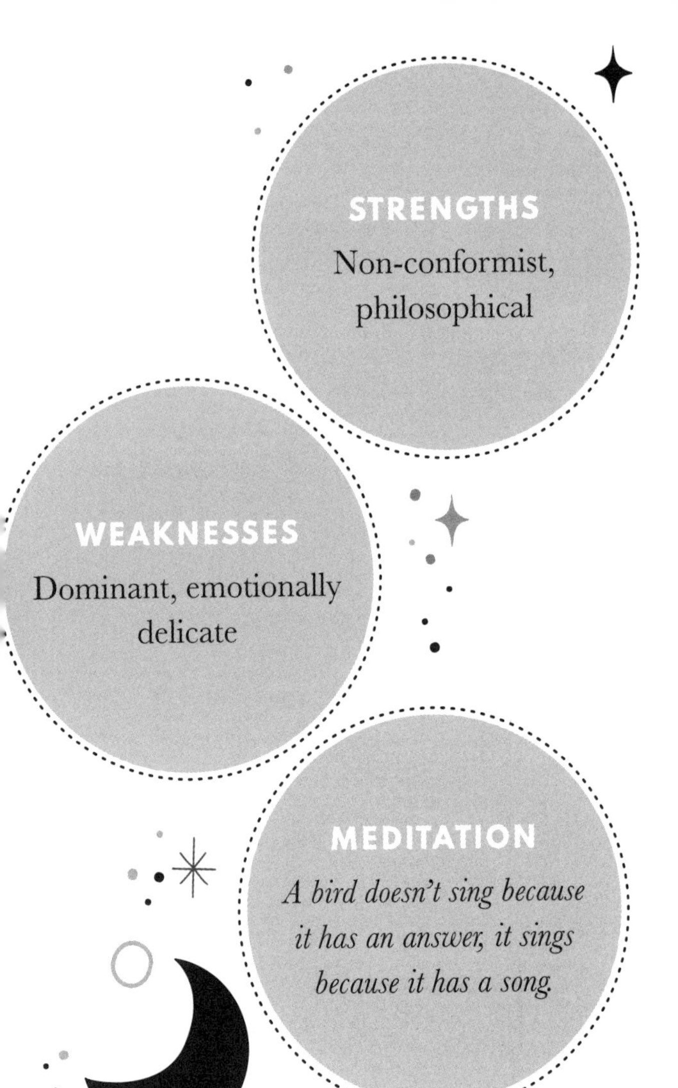

STRENGTHS

Non-conformist, philosophical

WEAKNESSES

Dominant, emotionally delicate

MEDITATION

A bird doesn't sing because it has an answer, it sings because it has a song.

9 November

You are a self-dramatizing and forceful person with a lot to say – there is never a dull moment when you're around. You take risks, love to gamble for high stakes and have a lust for extreme adventure. You have wide-ranging interests and cannot bear to be pinned down by one thing or one person. Your life is lived on a broad canvas that inspires less confident people. Your problem is when you adopt a 'holier-than-thou' attitude which comes from your fervent belief to improve yourself and others. You are loyal and generous to those you love and your word is your bond. In love you need someone who is willing to explore life with you, and is content to let you go off on your own travels. Gliding is a perfect sport for you, as you love flying and seeing the big picture.

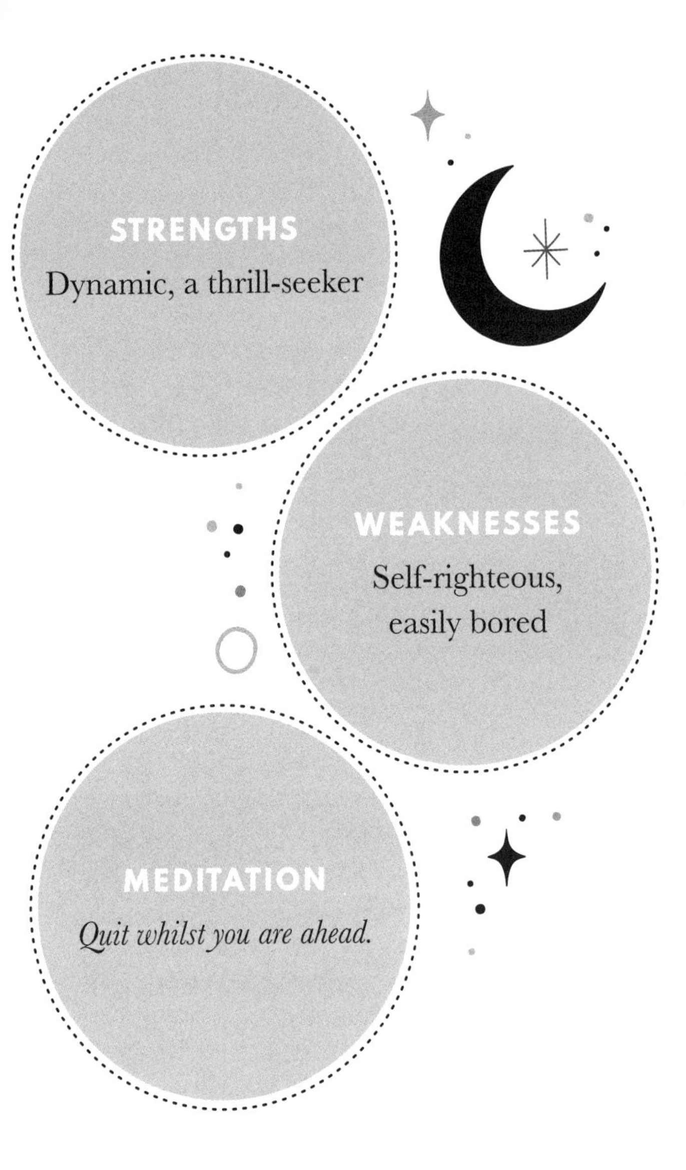
STRENGTHS
Dynamic, a thrill-seeker
WEAKNESSES
Self-righteous,
easily bored
MEDITATION
Quit whilst you are ahead.

10 November

You are a purposeful and ambitious person. From early on in life you know what you want to achieve and set your sights high. You have the ability to tackle difficult issues, and with your strong moral and physical courage, you usually succeed. If, however, you fail and get overlooked on your way to the top, your frustration can create health issues. You are adept at regeneration and can transform raw materials into 'gold', whether it's a building, a company, or yourself. You are a pragmatic person but will not compromise your principles. This can lead to others seeing you as being inflexible. Relationships are serious for you, and you marry for love and financial security. Relaxation is vital for your emotional well-being. Your lack of flexibility would be remedied by a freestyle jazz dance form.

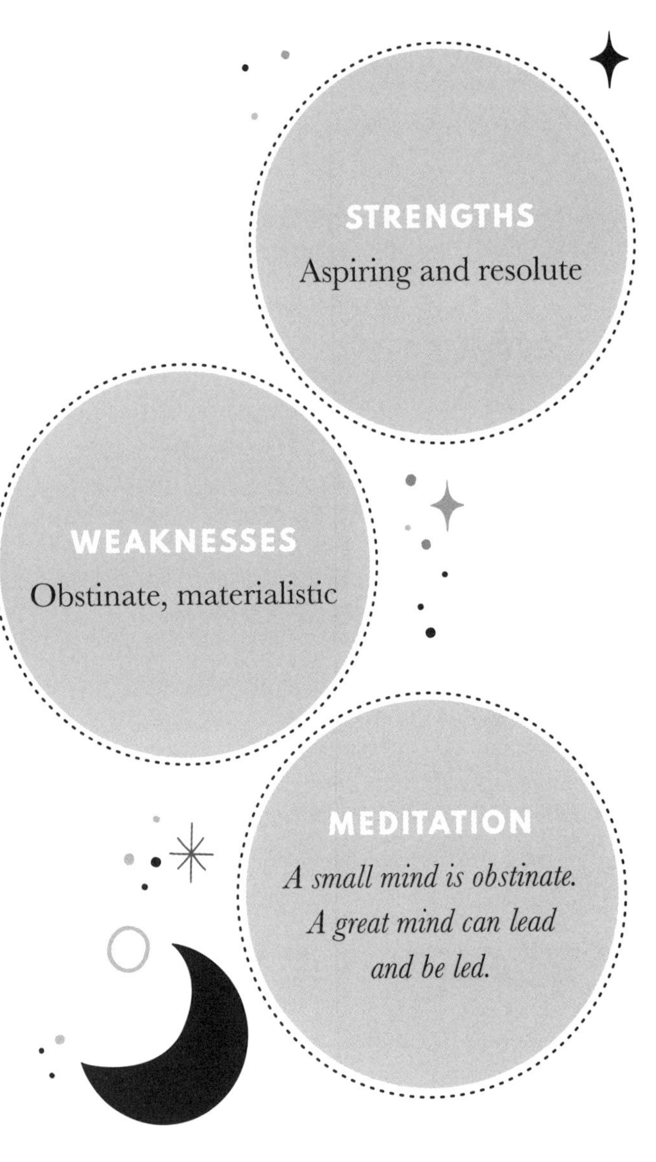
STRENGTHS
Aspiring and resolute
WEAKNESSES
Obstinate, materialistic
MEDITATION
A small mind is obstinate.
A great mind can lead
and be led.

11 November

You are an eccentric and unconventional person who needs a great deal of personal freedom. You love to shock people with your controversial views on life and have a way of delivering your ideas with power and passion. You can be deeply interested in the environment and will campaign on issues such as global warming. You love innovation and will be the first to buy a hybrid car or install solar panels in your roof. You are not traditional, and your life has to contain an edgy drama of danger and constant change. You are not naturally monogamous and when young you can embrace the idea of 'free love', however, you end up discovering just how jealous you can be! As you get older this becomes more an idea than a reality as you learn to appreciate intellectual companionship.

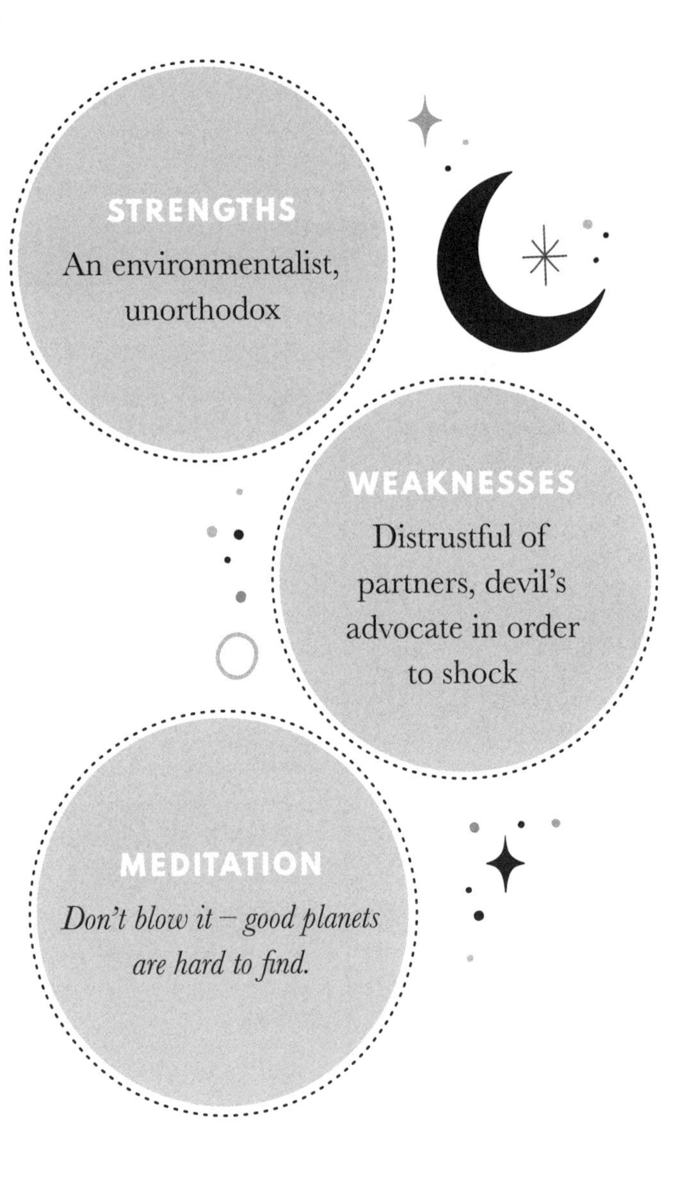

STRENGTHS

An environmentalist, unorthodox

WEAKNESSES

Distrustful of partners, devil's advocate in order to shock

MEDITATION

Don't blow it – good planets are hard to find.

12 November

You are a person who is in touch with the deepest dreams of the collective. You can create a vision that has power and a mesmerizing intensity that has qualities of a fairytale or myth. This you do by your art, or your life itself – you are truly memorable and never forgotten. You are sensitive and deeply emotional, and at times can get overwhelmed by a huge sense of sadness at the suffering you see in the world. You can be quite inconsolable and are prone to addictions, until you learn to channel these feelings into your creativity. Your relationships are the stuff of great dramas, with intense highs and lows. You need a partner who is willing to stand by you and share the emotions with you. You adore the movies and a good old-fashioned romantic epic such as *Gone with the Wind* is food for your soul.

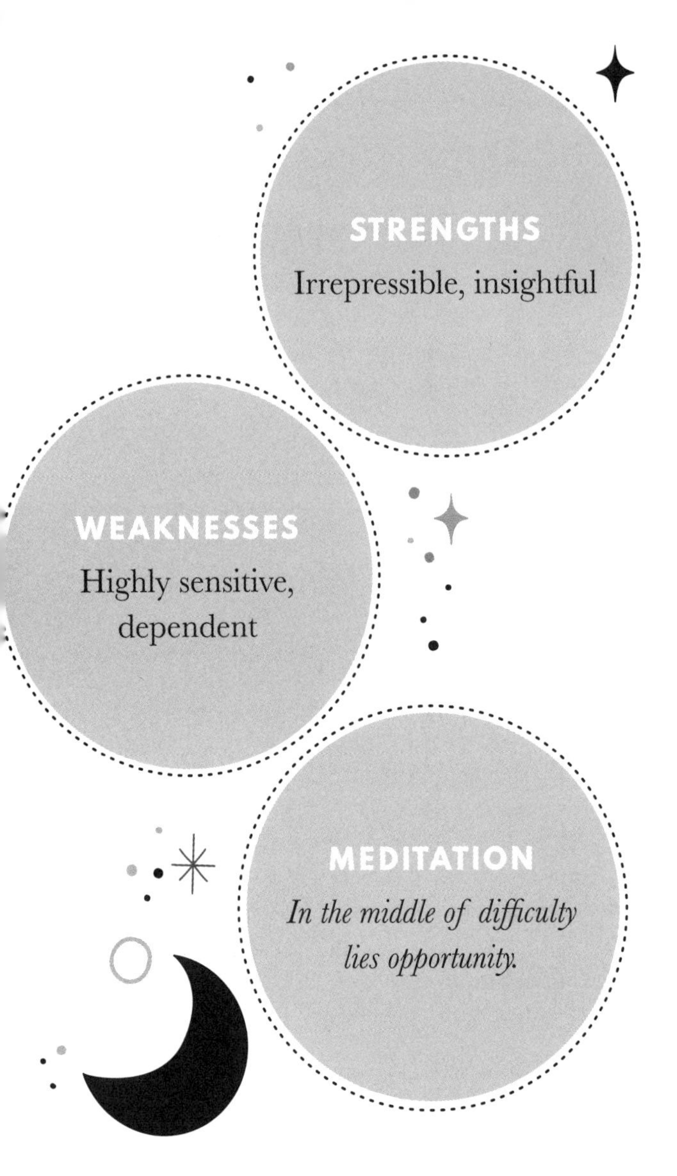

STRENGTHS

Irrepressible, insightful

WEAKNESSES

Highly sensitive, dependent

MEDITATION

In the middle of difficulty lies opportunity.

13 November

You are a charismatic and intense person with deep emotions. Due to your sensitive and perceptive nature, you have the ability to tap into the mood of the people and deliver what they want. This can be through your creative gifts as a writer, actor or healer. You are very ambitious and want to make your mark on the world from a very young age. You have a shrewd and canny mind and do well in business, especially in the stock market, as you have finely honed intuition. Relationships can be an emotional roller-coaster, so you need a grounded partner who isn't easily put off by your volatile moods. However, negative emotions can take over and you can sink into the depths of self-pity. Homeopathy would be worth exploring as a way of healing and restoring emotional balance.

STRENGTHS
Intuitive, determined
WEAKNESSES
Overwhelmed by negativity and, at times, self-absorbed
MEDITATION
Make others feel good about themselves in order to feel good about yourself.

14 November

You are a golden person with innate glamour and bewitching charm. You also have a penchant for investigating the darker aspects of life. With a strong appetite for sex, money, and power, you find it difficult to compromise. When pushed you stand up for what you believe in, even if it is the unpopular choice. This propels you towards centre stage, a place of leadership where you belong, and yet there is reluctance, as you fear being so exposed. You are incredibly hard-working and give yourself wholeheartedly to any project you believe in. You can be a snob and intolerant of those who disagree with your deeply-held principles. Your partner needs to look good by your side, yet not to steal the spotlight from you. Ease off work and leave time for play and having fun.

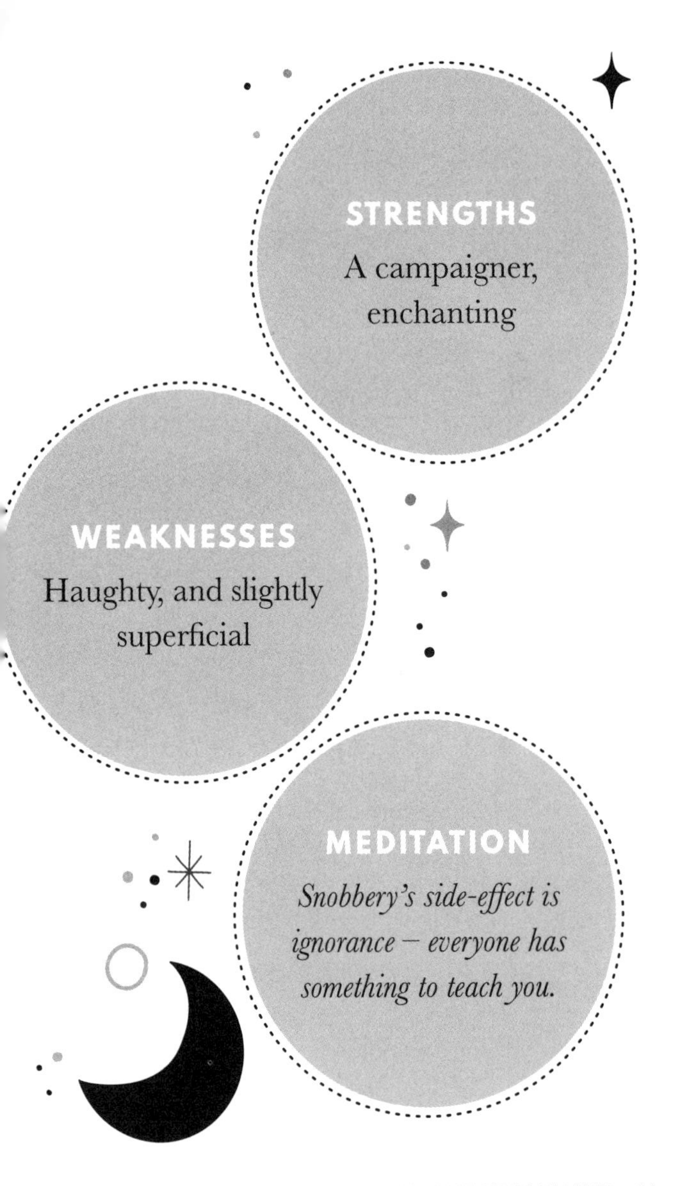
STRENGTHS
A campaigner, enchanting
WEAKNESSES
Haughty, and slightly superficial
MEDITATION
Snobbery's side-effect is ignorance – everyone has something to teach you.

15 November

You are an intelligent person with a sharp mind and quick wit. You are a superb organizer and planner with a clear methodical approach. You can be ruthless, which is great when clearing out clutter as you have an ability to discard what is no longer useful. However, because you can get caught in every detail, you are apt to see, and point out, the faults of others. You have good technical skills and tremendous physical stamina so sport is a likely profession. You can win against all odds as you have great determination. In relationships you need passion and also security – not easy to find in one person. Plus you can over-organize and control your partner, which is not conducive to happiness. Perfecting your body gives you huge satisfaction so weight training or yoga has immense appeal.

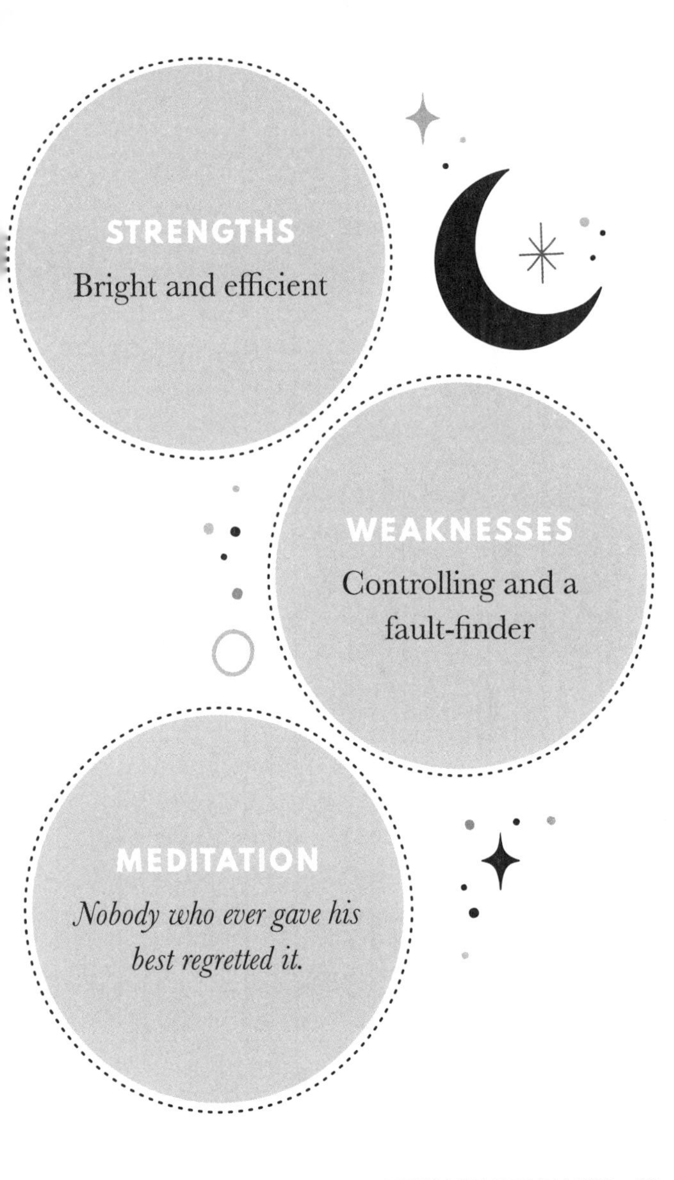

STRENGTHS

Bright and efficient

WEAKNESSES

Controlling and a fault-finder

MEDITATION

Nobody who ever gave his best regretted it.

16 November

You are a charming and delightful person with a quiet ambition and ideals to make the world a better place. You have impeccable good manners and always say the right thing, complimenting and appreciating people. With expensive taste you buy the best and can easily overspend as you cannot bear to have anything ugly around you. However, you are not weak, there is a core of steel within you and you can apply pressure when needed. Your work takes second place to your personal life and you tend to view marriage as an alliance. You are sensitive and intuitively know what your partner is feeling and what they need. You can be possessive and tend to get jealous if your partner doesn't pay enough attention to you. Restore the romance with a candlelit dinner.

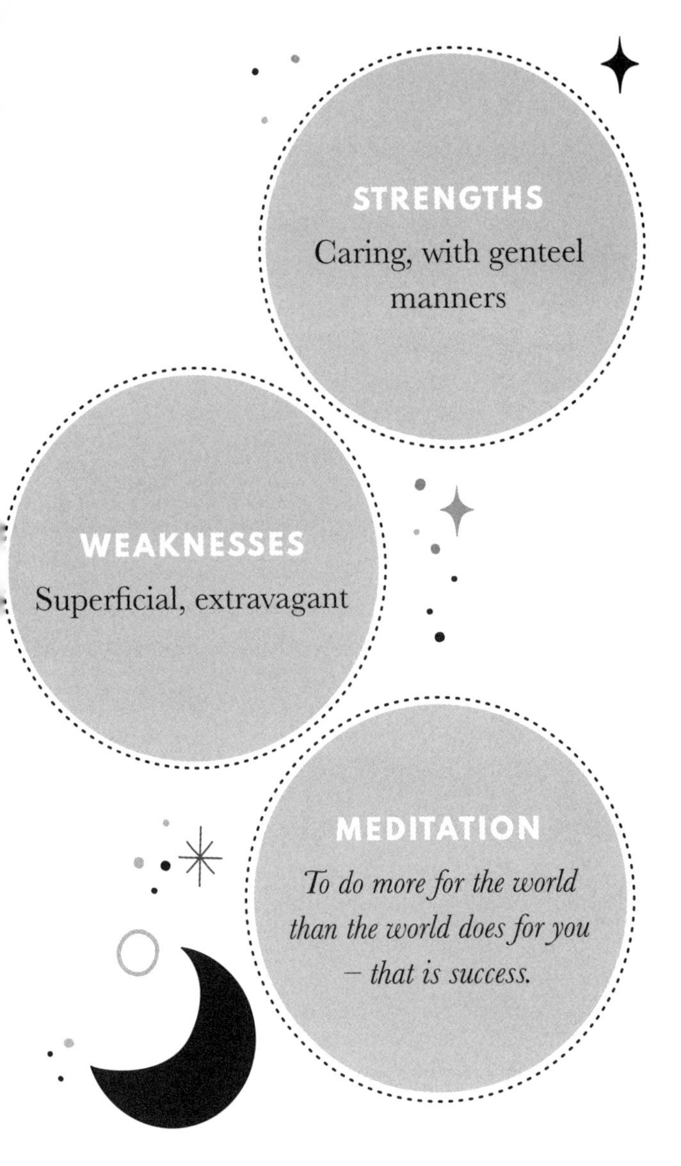

STRENGTHS

Caring, with genteel manners

WEAKNESSES

Superficial, extravagant

MEDITATION

To do more for the world than the world does for you – that is success.

17 November

You are an enigma, someone that only a few really know but all respect. You can be very secretive and suspicious. However, you are to be saluted as you have endured many struggles in your life and come through shining. Your heart is strong and you have developed enormous faith and optimism. Exploring the dark side of life fascinates you, and you revel in horror or occult stories. You have a keen intelligence and make astute judgements on situations and people. Nothing gets past your eagle eyes. Medical research, detective work and forensics all suit you. Emotionally you have strong desires and need for intimacy, so thrive in a committed relationship. Your partner needs to be someone you respect and your true equal. You need an active game such as squash where you let your emotions out.

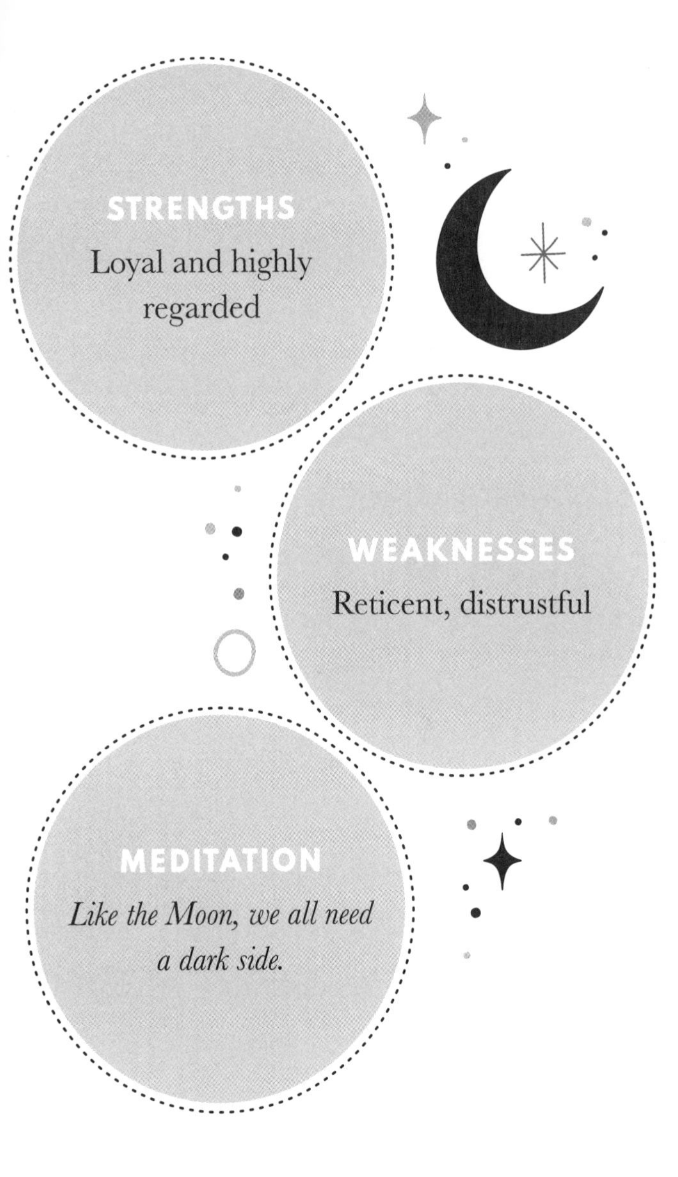
STRENGTHS
Loyal and highly regarded
WEAKNESSES
Reticent, distrustful
MEDITATION
Like the Moon, we all need a dark side.

18 November

You are a crusader, a person with an investigative mind. You are a fervent supporter of any cause you believe in. You can be restless in your search for the ultimate truth. You study many subjects – astronomy, psychology, philosophy and theology but until you find a spiritual path you can feel unfulfilled. You tend to rush forward without proper planning and can get careless and metaphorically tread on people's toes. You adore sports that challenge and stretch you physically and emotionally. You have a passion for the theatre and make a great impresario or backer for a musical. Your lover is also your companion with your partner following your lead. Later in your life romance matters less to you than a spiritual connection. Opera helps you transcend daily life and is the ideal way for you to elevate any bad mood.

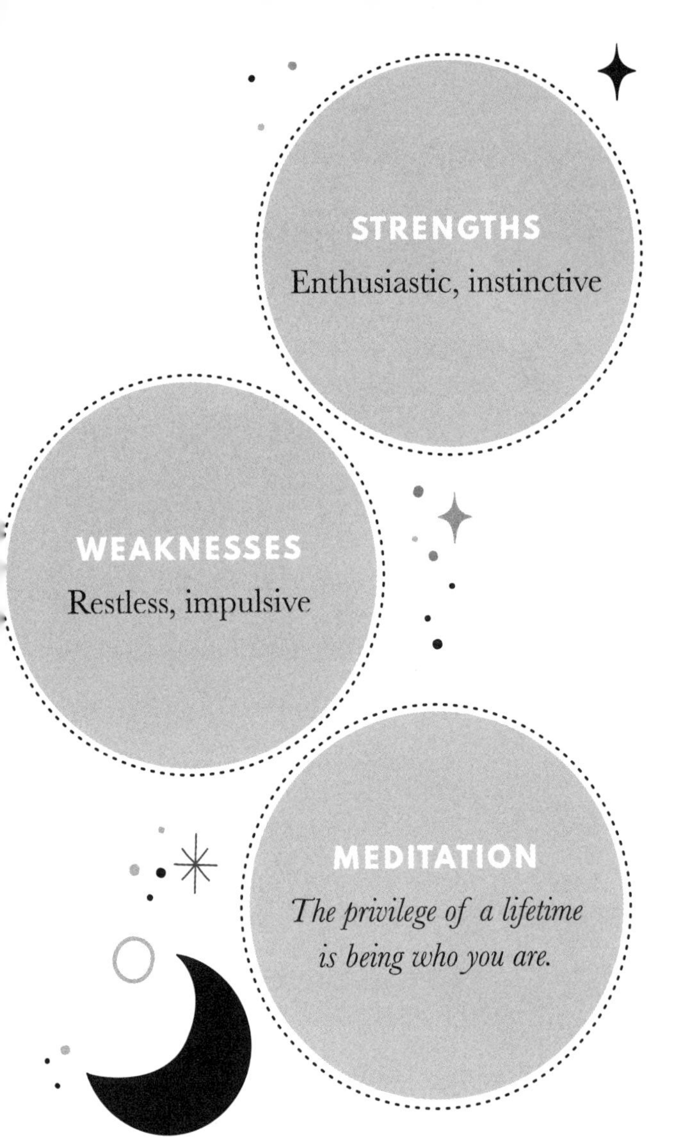
STRENGTHS
Enthusiastic, instinctive
WEAKNESSES
Restless, impulsive
MEDITATION
The privilege of a lifetime is being who you are.

19 November

You are a tenacious and committed person. You have a dark brooding intensity which makes you stand out from the crowd. With your fine rational intellect and thoughtful attitude, you have been seen as an old soul since your youth. You are most happy when you are working hard and you constantly set yourself new challenges. You fit well into society's hierarchy and your aim is to win and get to the top. Your weakness is a tendency for cynicism and evaluating everything on the physical level. You treat your love life as a project and you take time before you give yourself wholeheartedly. You tend to worry and get weighed down with responsibilities. Humour is your biggest asset and this gives you a much-needed release for your energy. Playing practical jokes on your unsuspecting friends brings childlike joy.

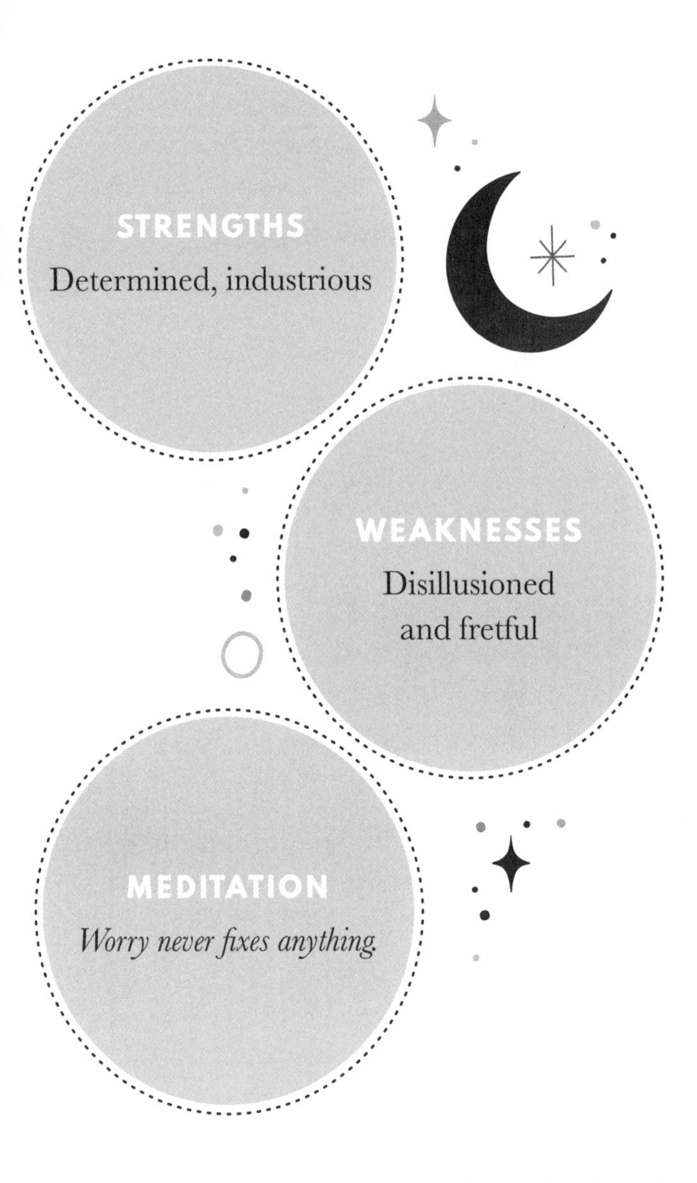
STRENGTHS
Determined, industrious
WEAKNESSES
Disillusioned
and fretful
MEDITATION
Worry never fixes anything.

20 November

You are a person with a quiet strength, determination and a deep concern for others. You have an overwhelming desire to live a useful life and to be of practical service to the world. You have a great deal of common sense and are totally dependable; a true friend that others rely upon. You are sensitive to people's emotional problems and are drawn to the caring and healing professions. You are also fascinated by renovation and are quite prepared to roll up your sleeves and get involved with a rebuilding project. Your relationships are either all or nothing and you can spend a long time alone until you meet the right person, however, you can be very possessive and controlling which drives people away. Gardening is very nurturing for you and gets you in touch with the cycles of life.

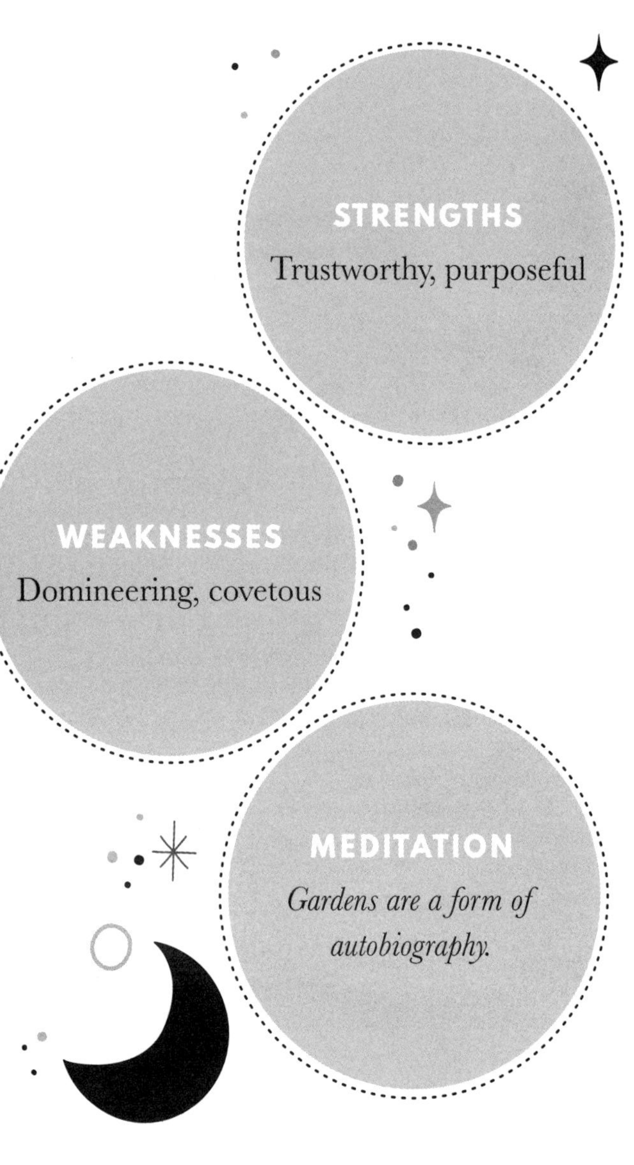
STRENGTHS
Trustworthy, purposeful
WEAKNESSES
Domineering, covetous
MEDITATION
Gardens are a form of autobiography.

21 November

You are a mystery, a person who at first can appear light-hearted and flirtatious, yet are also as deep and unfathomable as the ocean. You have a powerful imagination and are highly creative. You have an active and busy mind, always learning something new and you excel at being an educator. You are always on the phone connecting with your wide network and love passing on information – the role of the gossip columnist fits you like a glove! In love, you tend to have several affairs going at once, yet somehow you can get away with it due to your inordinate charm. If married, you need an easy-going and practical partner who can inspire you and not worry about never fully understanding you. You are the eternal student – so someone whom you respect and takes the role of teacher is your best ally.

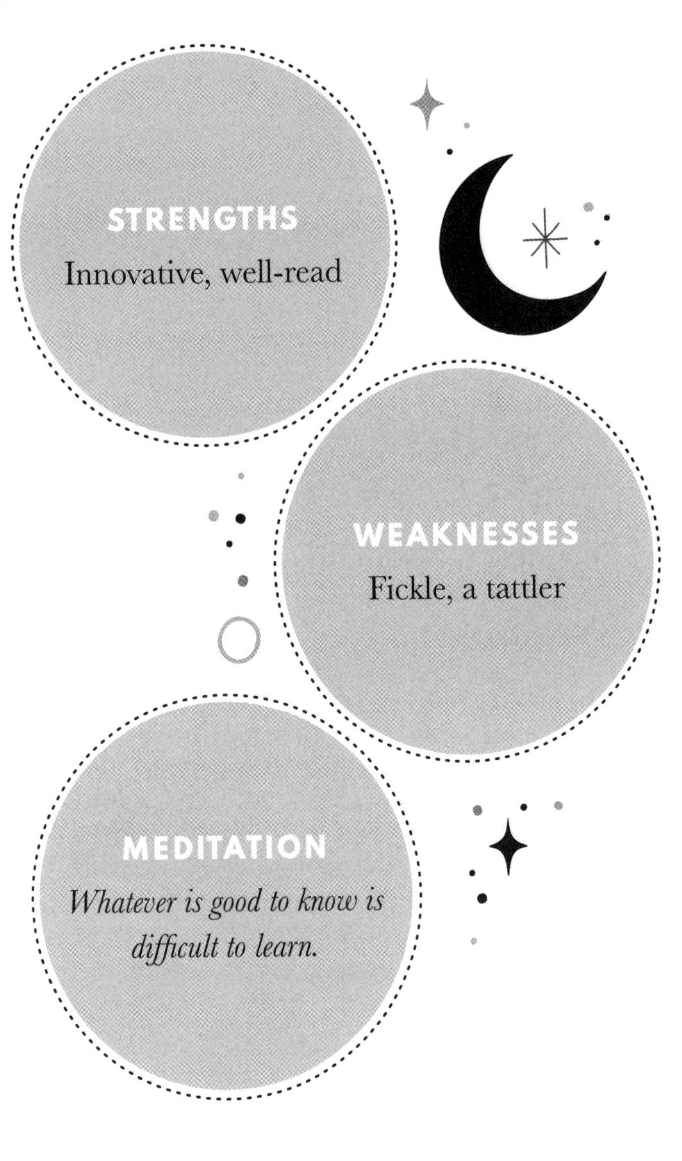
STRENGTHS
Innovative, well-read
WEAKNESSES
Fickle, a tattler
MEDITATION
Whatever is good to know is difficult to learn.

22 November

You are an imaginative and sincere person with a strong sense of self. Emotionally resilient and compassionate, you can be very protective. You fiercely care for and mother people, especially children and the underprivileged. This draws you into the caring professions where you can rise to a top managerial position. You are not intimidated by people, whatever their status, and quite enjoy a fight as you revel in deep emotions. A position of power suits you as others feel they can lean and depend on you. Your relationships are complex – you are loyal and steadfast, but you can also be demanding and clingy. Family life can be richly rewarding as you long to recreate the perfect childhood. Bach Flower Remedies are ideally suited to you when you become stressed and over-emotional.

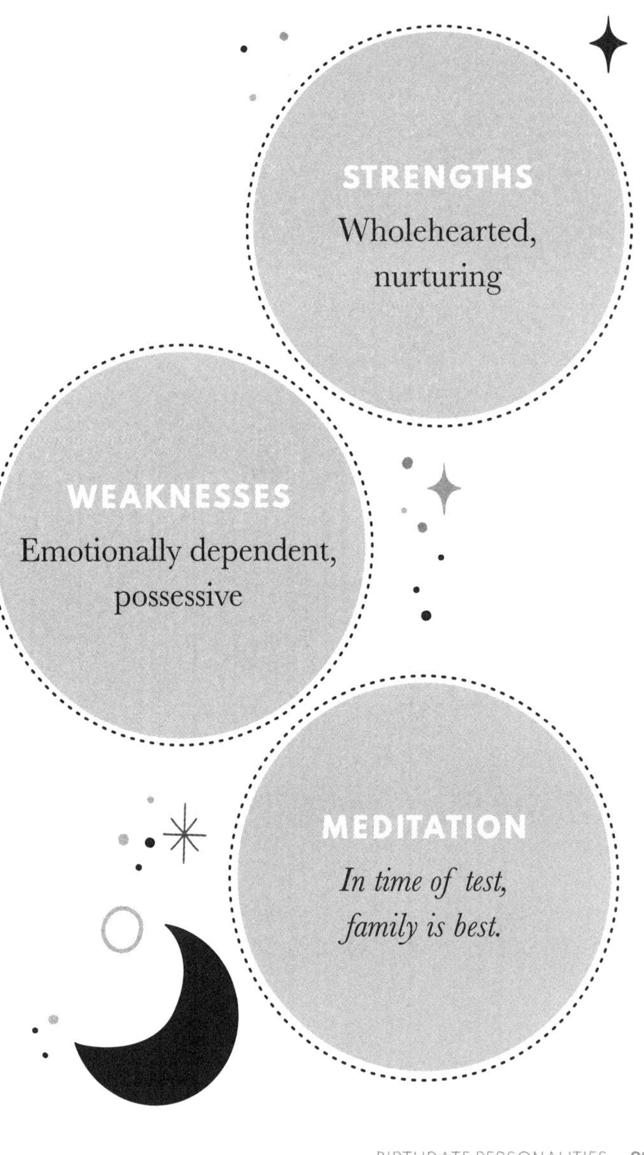

STRENGTHS

Wholehearted, nurturing

WEAKNESSES

Emotionally dependent, possessive

MEDITATION

In time of test, family is best.

Going
DEEPER

Astrology has
more to give than just
your Sun sign ... learn to
read the complexities
in your personal
birth chart.

Your personal birth chart

Understanding your Sun sign is an essential part of astrology, but it's the tip of the iceberg. To take your astrological wisdom to the next level, you'll need a copy of your unique birth chart – a map of the heavens for the precise moment you were born. You can find your birth chart at the Free Horoscopes link at: www.astro.com.

ASTROLOGICAL SYNTHESIS

When you first explore your chart you'll find that as well as a Sun sign, you also have a Moon sign, plus a Mercury, Venus, Mars, Jupiter, Saturn, Neptune, Uranus and Pluto sign - and that they all mean something different. Then there are astrological houses to consider, ruling planets and Rising signs, aspects and element types – all of which you will learn more about in the birth chart section on pages 112–115.

The art to astrology is in synthesising all this intriguing information to paint a picture of someone's character, layer by layer. Now that you understand your Scorpio Sun personality better, it's time to go deeper, and to look at the next layer – your Moon sign. To find your own Moon sign go to pages 104–111.

THE MOON'S INFLUENCE

After the Sun, your Moon sign is the second biggest astrological influence in your birth chart. It describes your emotional nature – your feelings, instincts and moods, and how you respond to different sorts of people and situations. By blending your outer, Scorpio Sun character with your inner, emotional, Moon sign, you'll get a much more balanced picture. If you don't feel that you're 100% Scorpio, your Moon sign will probably explain why!

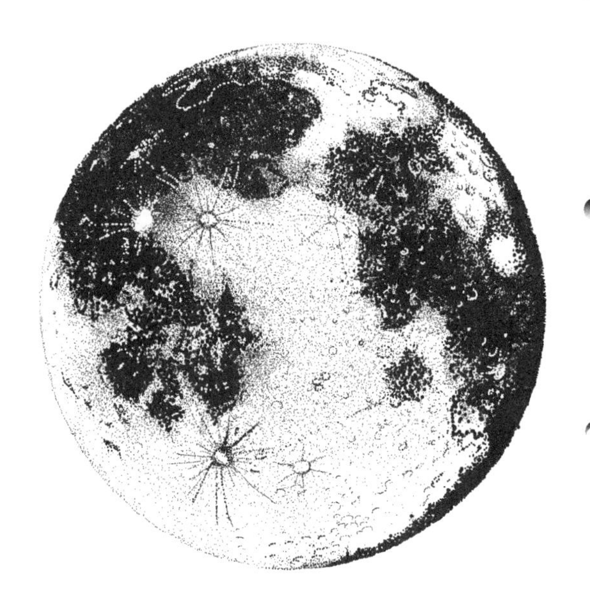

Scorpio with Moon signs

SCORPIO SUN/**ARIES MOON**

You're a powerhouse of physical and emotional energy. Your Mars-ruled Moon could mean you have a sharp temper, but it usually vanishes as speedily as it arrived. You're driven to succeed, and you don't hold back. Where others fall by the wayside, you're still fuelled by a mysterious, burning passion that always gets you where you want to be. This relentless drive can be a little overpowering for any potential new partner. You can be a little feisty in your closest relationships but when people get to know you, they realise you are an extremely loyal and loving person who needs a strong-willed partner to conquer the world with.

SCORPIO SUN/**TAURUS MOON**

Scorpio and Taurus are opposite signs, meaning you were born on a full Moon. Your placid, sensual Taurus Moon is unwavering and dislikes change. You won't be keen on leaving your emotional comfort zone. And your Scorpio Sun doesn't want to use up emotional energy on trivial matters. But you don't shy away from making deep, transformational adjustments on a psychological level. You seek emotional and financial stability from a partner and you're a considerate lover, though you can become jealous if provoked. You're not impulsive, you think things through carefully before deciding on a course of action, but when you make a move, you have the fortitude to pull yourself out of whatever trouble you find yourself in, draw a line, and start afresh. Taurus Moon people usually have pleasant voices and musical ability, and the creative arts will help you express your emotional energy.

SCORPIO SUN/**GEMINI MOON**

Where your light-hearted Gemini Moon softens your emotional intensity, it magnifies your intellectual curiosity. You tend to become fascinated with subjects or ideas, obsessively study them, then after you know how it all works you move on to the next intriguing subject. This can also be applied to your close personal relationships, which can consume your every waking thought for months or even years, and then once you think you have got to the bottom of the mystery, you lose interest. One job, one hobby or one romance isn't usually enough to hold your attention for long, which is why your romantic liaisons are often unconventional in some way. You need freedom in your partnerships and may live in a separate house, or even another country, to your partner.

SCORPIO SUN/**CANCER MOON**

A shrewd and complex character, you are highly protective of the people you love, and rarely reveal your inner thoughts to people you don't know. You're witty and clever and often very successful in business. But you're something of a dark horse. Alluring and intelligent, you won't be short of admirers, but once you have committed to someone you remain passionately loyal. Your home life and family are exceedingly important to you, and that's where you are able to relax and freely express yourself. Romantically, you can be initially shy or overly cautious but you're so intuitive that you will usually know on an instinctive level whether the relationship will work or not. Serious, sincere, but passionate, you look for a partner who is emotionally intelligent and mature.

SCORPIO SUN/**LEO MOON**

Dynamic and friendly you put a great deal of energy into everything you do. You have an air of authority and are nobody's fool. Emotionally you are playful, creative and attention-seeking, and in return you are faithful, open and loyal. You're an assertive person, keen to show yourself in the best possible light, and you have a knack for making other people feel good about themselves, too. You're not frightened of making large-scale changes in your life and work intensively to reach your ambitions. You need an encouraging partner, someone who will sing your praises and cheer you on from the side-lines. In return you'll place your lover at the centre of your life and will do all you can to keep the passion and fun side of the relationship burning brightly.

SCORPIO SUN/**VIRGO MOON**

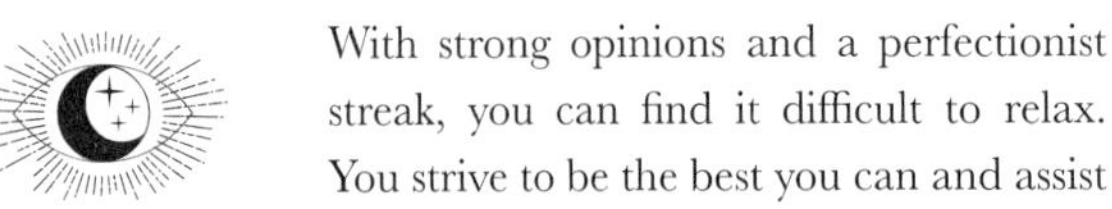

With strong opinions and a perfectionist streak, you can find it difficult to relax. You strive to be the best you can and assist others to reach the stars. Teaching, science, writing or accountancy would be a suitable career where you can focus on the details of any logical, practical work. If you're not intellectually challenged, you may become critical of others, and particularly harsh on yourself. You have uncanny intuition and sense things in others that they find difficult to communicate. Romantically you can be self-conscious and work best with a partner who will be able to draw out your considerable talents. You need warmth and compassion, otherwise you may become emotionally inhibited and obsessed with unimportant details, rather than seeing the full picture.

SCORPIO SUN/**LIBRA MOON**

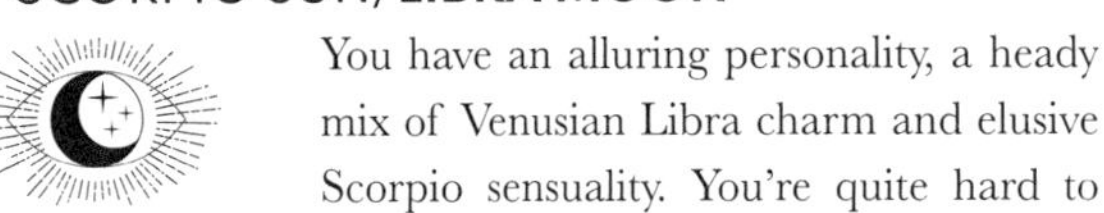

You have an alluring personality, a heady mix of Venusian Libra charm and elusive Scorpio sensuality. You're quite hard to resist when you want something. You're a born flatterer, skilled in making people feel better about themselves, even if what you're saying is not always completely true! Strong-willed and charismatic, you put enormous energy into making your world more peaceful and beautiful. With your Pluto/Venus combination, you have refined, if stark, tastes, and you would probably enjoy a career as an architect or as a graphic designer. Looking for someone to share your life reflects your Libran desire to feel 'whole' through partnership with another. And your Scorpio intensity and sex drive means you need an ardent, emotionally fulfilling love life and an active social life together.

SCORPIO SUN/**SCORPIO MOON**

Born at a new Moon, you are a double Scorpio. Although you hunger for emotional depth, on the surface you can appear remarkably poised and self-controlled. But your strength, determination and apparent detachment conceal what can be seething passion, rage or jealousy. You're a master at hiding your true feelings, as you fear your nakedness exposes you to others' manipulation. Because you give yourself so completely when you're in love, if you are betrayed you feel the pain at the core of your being. This is not something you deal with lightly. It's your craving for real, powerful intimacy that causes your 'sex-crazed' Scorpio myth. And to stop from feeling taken advantage of, you'll use whatever secrets or emotional ammunition at your disposal to protect yourself.

SCORPIO SUN/**SAGITTARIUS MOON**

You are a strong-willed, passionate and freedom-loving individual. Your Scorpio Sun personality shines when you go deep – and in philosophical Sagittarius you look to experience intellectual and adventurous pursuits. You like to experiment and explore what you are made of. You'll push your own boundaries and challenge those of the people who want to feel close to you. You thrive in an intellectually and emotionally stimulating relationship where you can experience extremes and come out stronger and more resilient than before. To experience the heights, you have to sometimes also explore the depths, but that's a price you think is worth paying. Knowledge is your power!

SCORPIO SUN/**CAPRICORN MOON**

Your Pluto-ruled Sun and Saturn ruled Moon are the markers of a capable and responsible person. Your Capricorn Moon means you are likely to be ambitious – and with your Plutonian self-discipline backing you up, not much can stand in the way of you getting what you want. You may work a little too much and have a rather serious disposition, but even from a young age you probably understood that to get what you want in life you have to have a watertight plan. Emotionally, you may appear standoffish, but this is more out of self-preservation than fear of commitment. The opposite, in fact, is more likely the case, where you may long for love, but don't take your feelings, or anyone else's lightly. When someone suitable does come along you're one of the most devoted people imaginable.

SCORPIO SUN/**AQUARIUS MOON**

Scorpio Sun people can appear detached from their emotions, but this is usually a facade to protect themselves against people who might use their feelings against them. But with an Aquarius Moon, your emotional side is tempered, and you'll be happier in social situations, making friends more easily and sharing many interests with people with unusual views on life. Although you are tolerant with the people you care about, you have the Scorpio tenacity to fight for what you believe in. Nobody wants to get on the wrong side of you in an argument! You are a bright, intellectual soul who is rarely bored, and seek a partner who can keep you on your toes intellectually while providing the emotional security that most Scorpios are too scared to admit they need!

SCORPIO SUN/**PISCES MOON**

A double Water sign your Pluto/Neptune combination creates an intuitive and instinctive personality. You empathise with how others are feeling, with an almost mystical ability to understand the human soul. An artistic lifestyle suits you best where you can express your feelings freely through colour, design, music or theatre. A born romantic, you have big dreams of the perfect love and have probably rather haphazardly bumped up against a disappointing reality enough times to have learned not to count your chickens before they've hatched. You're a thoughtful and sensitive partner who picks up energies from other people, so your partner should be one as gentle and impressionable as you are.

Birth charts

Learning about your Sun and Moon sign opens the gateway into exploring your own birth chart. This snapshot of the skies at the moment of someone's birth is as complex and interesting as the person it represents. Astrologers the world over have been studying their own birth charts, and those of people they know, their whole lives and still find something new in them every day. There are many schools of astrology and an inexhaustible list of tools and techniques, but here are the essentials to get you started ...

ZODIAC SIGNS AND PLANETS

These are the keywords for the 12 zodiac signs and the planets associated with them, known as ruling planets.

ARIES

courageous, bold, aggressive, leading, impulsive

Ruling planet

MARS

shows where you take action and how you channel your energy

TAURUS

reliable, artistic, practical, stubborn, patient

Ruling planet

VENUS

describes what you value and who and what you love

GEMINI

clever, friendly, superficial, versatile

Ruling planet

MERCURY

represents how your mind works and how you communicate

CANCER

emotional, nurturing, defensive, sensitive

Ruling planet

MOON

describes your emotional needs and how you wish to be nurtured

LEO

confidence, radiant, proud, vain, generous

Ruling planet

SUN

your core personality and character

VIRGO
analytical, organised, meticulous, thrifty

Ruling planet
MERCURY
co-ruler of Gemini and Virgo

LIBRA
fair, indecisive, cooperative, diplomatic

Ruling planet
VENUS
co-ruler of Taurus and Libra

SCORPIO
regenerating, magnetic, obsessive, penetrating

Ruling planet
PLUTO
deep transformation, endings and beginnings

SAGITTARIUS
optimistic, visionary, expansive, blunt, generous

Ruling planet
JUPITER
travel, education and faith in a higher power

CAPRICORN

ambitious, responsible, cautious, conventional

Ruling planet

SATURN

your ambitions, work ethic and restrictions

AQUARIUS

unconventional, independent, erratic, unpredictable

Ruling planet

URANUS

where you rebel or innovate

PISCES

dreamy, chaotic, compassionate, imaginative, idealistic

Ruling planet

NEPTUNE

your unconscious, and where you let things go

The 12 houses

irth charts are divided into 12 sections, known as houses, each relating to different areas of life as follows:

FIRST HOUSE

associated with *Aries*

Identity – how you appear to others and your initial response to challenges

SECOND HOUSE

associated with *Taurus*

How you make and spend money, your talents, skills and how you value yourself

THIRD HOUSE

associated with *Gemini*

Siblings, neighbours, communication and short distance travel

FOURTH HOUSE

associated with *Cancer*

Home, family, your mother, roots and the past

FIFTH HOUSE

associated with *Leo*

Love affairs, romance, creativity, gambling and children

6
SIXTH HOUSE
associated with Virgo
Health, routines, organisation and pets
8
EIGHTH HOUSE
associated with Scorpio
Sex, death, transformation, wills and money you share with another
7
SEVENTH HOUSE
associated with Libra
Relationships, partnerships, others and enemies
9
NINTH HOUSE
associated with Sagittarius
Travel, education, religious beliefs, faith and generosity
10
TENTH HOUSE
associated with Capricorn
Career, father, ambitions, worldly success
11
ELEVENTH HOUSE
associated with Aquarius
Friends, groups, ideals and social or political movements
12
TWELFTH HOUSE
associated with Pisces
Spirituality, the unconscious mind, dreams and karma

THE ELEMENTS

Each zodiac sign belongs to one of the four elements – Earth, Air, Fire and Water – and these share similar characteristics.

EARTH	AIR
Taurus, Virgo, Capricorn	*Gemini, Libra, Aquarius*
Earth signs are practical, trustworthy, thorough and logical.	Air signs are clever, flighty, intellectual and charming.
FIRE	**WATER**
Aries, Leo, Sagittarius	*Cancer, Scorpio, Pisces*
Fire signs are active, creative, warm, spontaneous, innovators.	Water signs are sensitive, empathic, dramatic and caring.

PLANETARY ASPECTS

The aspects are geometric patterns formed by the planets and represent different types of energy. They are usually shown in two ways – in a separate grid or aspect grid and as the criss-crossing lines on the chart itself. There are oodles of different aspect patterns but to keep things simple we'll just be working with four: conjunctions, squares, oppositions and trines.

CONJUNCTION	**SQUARE**

0 degrees apart *intensifying*	90 degrees apart *challenging*
OPPOSITION	**TRINE**

180 degrees apart *polarising*	120 degrees apart *harmonising*

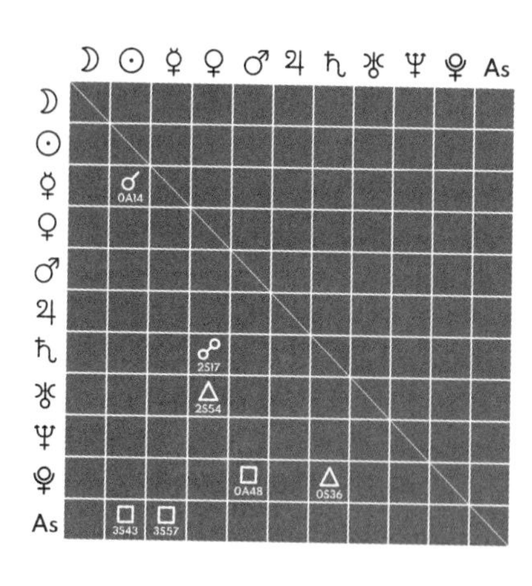

Planetary aspects for Cody's chart

HOUSES AND RISING SIGN

Each chart is a 360° circle, divided into 12 segments known as the houses (see pages 116–117 for house interpretations). The most important point in a birth chart is known as the Rising sign, which shows the zodiac sign on the Eastern horizon for the moment you were born. This is usually marked as AS or ASC on the chart drawing. This is the position from where the other houses and zodiac signs are drawn in a counter-clockwise direction. The Rising sign is always on the dividing line of the first house – the house associated with the self, how you appear to others, and the lens through which you view the world.

CHART RULER: The planetary ruler of a person's Rising zodiac sign is always a key player in unlocking a birth chart and obtaining a deeper understanding of it.

A SIMPLE BIRTH CHART INTERPRETATION FOR A SCORPIO SUN PERSON

BIRTH CHART FOR CODY BORN 2 NOVEMBER 1996 IN SHENZHEN, CHINA.

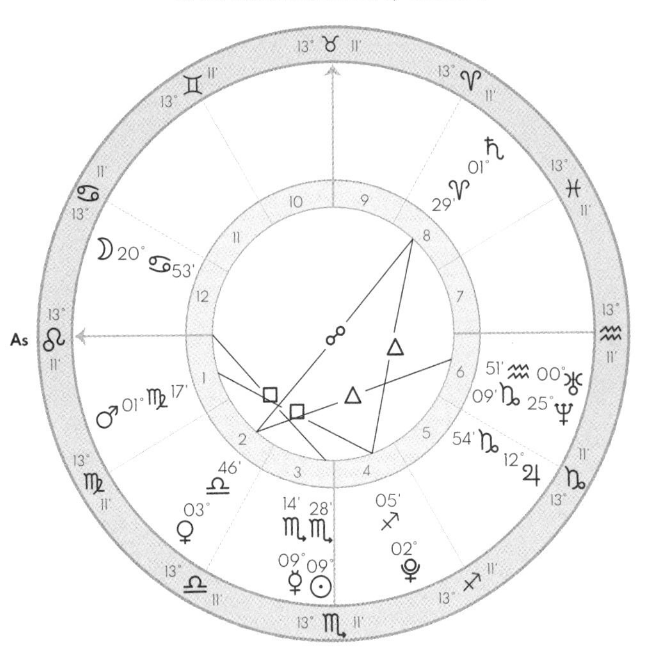

THE POSITION OF THE PLANETS: Cody has Leo Rising. The Sun and Mercury are in Scorpio and the Moon is Cancer. Venus is in Libra, Mars is in Virgo, Jupiter and Neptune occupy Capricorn, Saturn sits in Aries, Uranus is in Aquarius, and Pluto is in Sagittarius.

INTERPRETATION BASICS

As well as the signs the planets are in, you should note the houses that they sit in too. How do you begin to put all these signs and symbols together? It's usually best to begin with the Sun, Rising sign (As) and then to examine the condition of the Moon sign.

SUN, MOON, RISING SIGN AND CHART RULER: Cody's Sun and Mercury are in intense Scorpio in the third house of communication and thinking. Gemini is the ruler of the third house, so its placement is particularly strong. Cody ought to have a detective-like Scorpio desire to get to the bottom of any mystery, and he may enjoy writing or research. He'll probably be passionate and driven in getting the right message across.

His Moon is in home-loving Cancer, which shows a deeply caring and sensitive personality, and as it falls in his twelfth house, (dreams/imagination) he's probably very intuitive and artistic. Cody's Rising sign is ebullient, confident Leo, which will help him stand up for himself and he'll be sociable and cheerful. Cody's Rising sign ruler is the Sun, adding further weight to what is already a powerful third house, signifying Cody's lifelong thirst for knowledge.

OTHER PLANETS: Cody's Venus (relationships/money) is also auspicious, as it's in Libra (Venus jointly rules Taurus and Libra) and it's sitting in the second house, which is ruled by Taurus. Cody will have a strong need for relationships and enjoys others' company very much.

His abilities and talents will attract money and he will have an eye for beauty or may have artistic or musical ability. Mars is also in the house it rules (first) which bolsters Virgo's position here, suggesting Cody is a meticulous, discerning person, who feels strongly about health and his work routines. Jupiter (travel/luck/expansion) in the fifth house of creativity and fun, is in Capricorn (business/ambition). Cody might enjoy expanding (Jupiter) creative ideas (fifth) and turning them into viable work options (Capricorn).

Saturn in Aries suggests a business leader, and in the eighth house could be linked to investing time and money (Saturn) in other people's resources (eighth). Neptune and Uranus sit together in the sixth house of work, health and routines. Cody may use his imagination (Neptune) to change (Uranus) his health and keep his career skills sharp (sixth). Pluto (resources/emotional intensity) occupies Sagittarius (adventure) in the fourth house (home/family). Perhaps Cody has had transformative (Pluto) experiences while travelling (Sagittarius) with his family (fourth house), or at least there seems potential for this to be a reality at some point in his life.

ADDING IN THE PLANETARY ASPECTS

Let's take a brief look at the strongest aspects – the ones with the most exact angles or 'orbs' to the planetary degrees (the numbers next to the planets).

SUN CONJUNCT MERCURY, SQUARE RISING SIGN (AS): Cody expresses himself (Sun) in a talkative, ideas-driven way and enjoys keeping in touch with the people around him. His initial approach (Rising/As) to life's challenges is to take the lead (Sun) but his confidence may sometimes rub people up the wrong way (square).

VENUS OPPOSITE SATURN AND TRINE URANUS: Cody's relationships (Venus) could be very black and white (opposition) but they will also be positive (trine) catalysts for change (Uranus).

MARS SQUARE PLUTO: When Cody deals with (Mars) challenging situations (square) he will be powerfully driven (Pluto) to succeed.

SATURN TRINE PLUTO: Cody's responsibilities (Saturn) lead to transformational (Pluto) opportunities (trine).

YOUR JOB AS AN ASTROLOGER

The interpretation above is simplified to help you understand some of the nuts and bolts of interpretation. There are almost as many techniques and tools for analysing birth charts as there are people!

Remember when you're putting the whole thing together that astrology doesn't show negatives or positives. The planets represent potential and opportunities, rather than definitions set in stone. It's your job as an astrologer to use the planets' wisdom to blend and synthesise those energies to create the picture of a whole person.

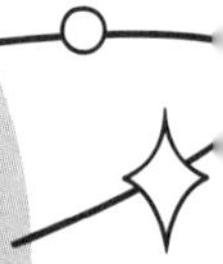

Going deeper

To see your own birth chart visit: www.astro.com and click the Free Horoscopes link and then enter your birth information. If you don't know what time you were born, put in 12.00pm. Your Rising sign and the houses might not be right, but the planets will be in the correct zodiac signs and the aspects will be accurate.

Further reading and credits

WWW.ASTRO.COM

This amazing astrological resource is extremely popular with both experienced and beginner astrologers. It's free to sign up and obtain your birth chart and personalised daily horoscopes.

BOOKS

PARKER'S ASTROLOGY by Derek and Julia Parker (Dorling Kindersley)

THE LITTLE BOOK OF ASTROLOGY by Marion Williamson (Summersdale)

THE BIRTHDAY ORACLE by Pam Carruthers (Arcturus)

THE 12 HOUSES by Howard Sasportas (London School of Astrology)

THE ARKANA DICTIONARY OF ASTROLOGY by Fred Gettings (Penguin)

THE ROUND ART by AJ Mann (Paper Tiger)

THE LUMINARIES by Liz Greene (Weiser)

SUN SIGNS by Linda Goodman (Pan Macmillan)

Marion Williamson is a best-selling astrology author and editor. *The Little Book of Astrology* and *The Little Book of the Zodiac* (Summersdale 2018) consistently feature in Amazon's top 20 astrology books. These were written to encourage beginners to move past Sun signs and delve into what can be a lifetime's study. Marion has been writing about different areas of self-discovery for over 30 years. A former editor of *Prediction* magazine for ten years, Marion had astrology columns in *TVTimes*, *TVEasy*, *Practical Parenting*, *Essentials* and *Anglers Mail* for over ten years. Twitter: @_I_am_astrology

Pam Carruthers is a qualified professional Vedic and Western astrologer and student of *A Course in Miracles*. An experienced Life Coach and Trainer, Pam helps clients discover the hidden patterns that are holding them back in their lives. A consultation with her is a life enhancing and healing experience. She facilitates a unique transformational workshop 'Healing your Birth Story' based on your birthchart. Based in the UK, Pam has an international clientele.

All images courtesy of Shutterstock and Freepik/ Flaticon.com.